That Patchwork Place®

Great Expectations

Houston, Texas

Karey Bresenhan
with Alice Kish and Gay Elliott McFarland

Dedication

This book is dedicated, with love and appreciation, to those without whom Great Expectations could never have become the shop it is today:

All those unknown quilters who left their unsigned quilts to inspire us.

Jewel Patterson, my mother, fourth generation Texas quilter, and senior quilting teacher at Great Expectations, who has given unstintingly of her love, talent, enthusiasm, hard work, support, and ideas.

All of the wonderful people who have worked and taught at Great Expectations in its twenty-one-year history and who have provided thousands of quilters with excellent service, good advice, and happy memories.

The staff of International Quilt Festival, which has pitched in to help the shop in so many ways whenever it was necessary.

All of the quilters who have honored Great Expectations by being loyal customers, eager learners, and true fabricoholics.

Special thanks to:

All the Great Expectations shop managers over the past twenty-one years, including Catherine Purifoy, Bev Harding, Nicki Becker, Georgianna Verbrugge, and Kim DeCoste; Kim DeCoste, Rachael Lambrecht, Lisa DeBee Schiller, and Harriet Rea for their help on samples and patterns; Pamela Lewis and Nancy O'Bryant for editing.

Credits

Editor-in-Chief .... Barbara Weiland
Managing Editor .... Greg Sharp
Technical Editor .... Janet White
Copy Editors .... Liz McGehee
                                          Stephanie Morton
Proofreader .... Leslie Phillips
Illustrator .... Brian Metz
Illustration Assistant .... Lisa McKenney
Photographer .... Brent Kane
Design Director .... Judy Petry
Text and Cover Designer .... Cheryl Stevenson
Production Assistant .... Claudia L'Heureux

Library of Congress Cataloguing-in-Publication Data

Bresenhan, Karey,
    Great Expectations, Houston, Texas / Karey Bresenhan with Alice Kish, Gay Elliott McFarland.
        p. cm. — (The New American quilt shop series)
    ISBN 1-56477-084-2
    1. Patchwork—Patterns. 2. Appliqué—Patterns. 3. Quilts—United States—History. 4. Great Expectations (Store) I. Kish, Alice. II. McFarland, Gay Elliott. III. Title. IV. Series.
TT835.B898   1995
746.46—dc20
                                          95-35153
                                               CIP

Great Expectations
© 1995 by Karey Bresenhan with Alice Kish and Gay Elliott McFarland
That Patchwork Place, Inc., PO Box 118, Bothell, WA 98041-0118 USA

Printed in the United States of America
00 99 98 97 96 95   6 5 4 3 2 1

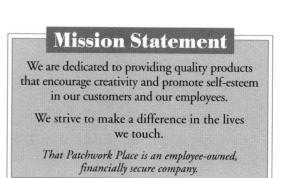

Mission Statement

We are dedicated to providing quality products that encourage creativity and promote self-esteem in our customers and our employees.

We strive to make a difference in the lives we touch.

That Patchwork Place is an employee-owned, financially secure company.

Table of Contents

*From the moment you enter the corporate
offices of Quilts, Inc., you realize how
special the organization is.*

Meet the Authors

Karey Bresenhan is the founder of Great Expectations Quilts. In Houston, Texas, she serves as president of Quilts, Inc., the parent company for International Quilt Festival, International Quilt Market, European Quilt Market, Quilt Expo, A Victorian Romance®, and Embellishment®. Karey is a co-founder of the Texas Sesquicentennial Quilt Association and of the Quilt Guild of Greater Houston. She is the co-author of *Lone Stars: A Legacy of Texas Quilts, 1836–1936*; *Lone Stars, Volume II, A Legacy of Texas Quilts, 1936–1986*; and *Hands All Around, Quilts from Many Nations*. She is also a co-founder of the American International Quilt Association, the only nonprofit, international quilt organization, and The Alliance for American Quilts. She is a fifth-generation Texas quilter and is a dedicated collector. Karey was inducted into the Quilter's Hall of Fame in the summer of 1995.

Alice Kish has been a quilter since 1973, when she lived in New Delhi, India, and admired a quilt owned by one of her American friends also stationed in India. She tried to reproduce her friend's Crazy quilt but couldn't figure out how it was done. When she spotted an article about quilting in *Redbook* magazine, with instructions, she was hooked!

When she and her husband, Tom, moved back to the States, she continued to quilt and hunt for appropriate fabrics from St. Louis to Omaha, from Cortez, Colorado, to Houston. When she moved to Houston in 1987, her goals were to find Great Expectations, join the Quilt Guild of Greater Houston, and attend International Quilt Festival. On a visit to Great Expectations, she noticed a Help Wanted sign, applied, and was hired on the spot! Alice, who still works in the store and assists with buying, also teaches classes for the shop. She has been on the Quilt Guild of Greater Houston's board since 1990. In 1994, she served as its president.

Her three children, Colin, Erin, and Nathan, grew up with quilts and consider Great Expectations a second home.

Gay Elliott McFarland is a writer and editor. She has worked in the Marketing Communications Division of Quilts, Inc., and continues to freelance for the company. Gay, who has a master's degree in creative writing, was a staff writer for *The Houston Chronicle* and *The Houston Post*; wrote a syndicated home furnishings column for ten years; and has written for numerous regional, national, and international publications. By avocation, she is a jewelry designer, and her work is found in museums and galleries. Gay is married to photographer Blair Pittman and they have one child, Slade.

(Left to right) Karey Bresenhan, Alice Kish, and Gay Elliott McFarland

About Great Expectations

Quilting and I go way back: My great-great-grandmother, Wilhelmina Schlack Uttech; my great-grandmother, Karoline Uttech Glaeser, after whom I'm named; my grandmothers, Ella Glaeser Pearce and Myrtle Loomis Patterson; and my mother, Jewel Pearce Patterson, preceded me in quilting and needle arts. I learned from those relatives, some of whom I never knew in person, by studying their tiny stitches and pondering their designs in the family's heirloom quilts. I learned from those I did know by example. "Sit here, thread your needle this way, and make your stitches just so." Long after people in other parts of the country had begun buying blankets from the nearest

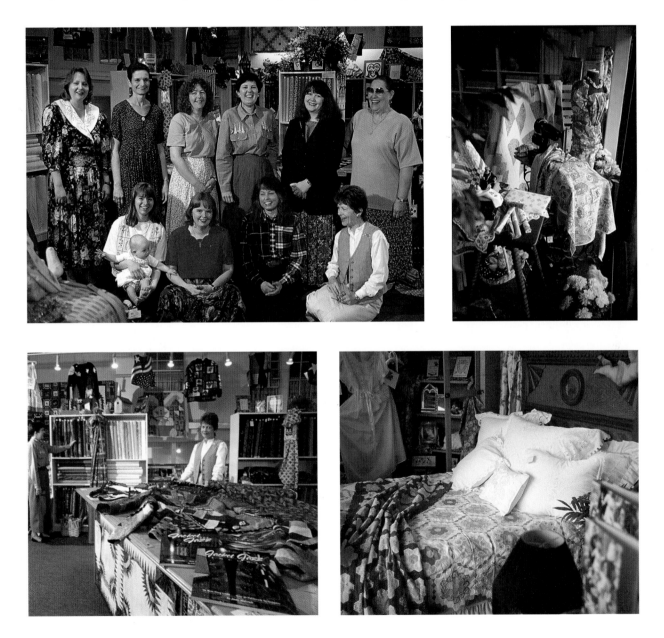

Great Expectations staff (top left). Standing, left to right: Jeni Beckstead, Mary Frances Barber, Kathy Wayne, Diana Crawley, Catherine Purifoy, Betty Eubank.
Sitting, left to right: Rachel Lambrecht and daughter, Hannah, Terry Stojan, Alice Kish, Harriet Rea.

Inspiration is waiting for all quilters at Great Expectations. Shop staff members and teachers—not to mention other quilters visiting the shop—are founts of quilting knowledge. The stock—fabrics, books, magazines, tools, displays, and classes—is a source for inspiration as well.

Sears & Roebuck, I was still attending family quilting bees.

I opened my quilt store, Great Expectations, in 1974 with a family heritage, a historical perspective—and zero retail experience. My lack of expertise was probably a blessing. I know it was a challenge.

The original Great Expectations store served as International Quilt Festival's first location. The shop has provided, and continues to provide, fabrics for raffle quilts, office space for nonprofit quilting organizations, financial support for fledgling projects, and a collection point for the quilts of the Texas Quilt Search and for the American International Quilt Association's (AIQA) annual judged show.

Great Expectations, like quilting itself, has changed and grown in the last twenty-one years. Once my mother taught *both* the classes—the beginner-level class and the advanced sampler class. Now we have many full-time teachers and several guest teachers each semester, along with a full brochure of classes, ranging from Jacket Jazz wearables to Mariner's Compass. Of course, we still offer beginner and sampler classes.

Great Expectations has been offering classes, advice, instruction, and inspiration for more than two decades. And the best is yet to come!

Karey Bresenhan

Shows that Grew from Great Expectations

International Quilt Festival is the largest annual quilt convention, show, sale, and quiltmaking academy in the world. More than 51,000 people from more than 25 foreign countries and all over the United States visited Quilt Festival during its four-day twentieth-anniversary show in 1994.

International Quilt Market showcases quilting supplies, fabrics, decorative crafts, textile art, needle crafts, art apparel, and dollmaking supplies. It is the only wholesale trade show in the world for the quilting and soft-crafts industry. With two shows per year in the United States, Quilt Market has been the primary catalyst for the development of the quilting industry around the world and an industry that now has sales exceeding $1.56 billion yearly.

European Quilt Market is the only wholesale trade show in Europe devoted to the quilting and soft-crafts industry. It has been held annually since 1988.

Quilt Expo is the only international consumer show for the quilting public and quilting retailers doing business in Europe; it is held in even-numbered years after the European Quilt Market. Expos have been held in Salzburg, Austria; Odense, Denmark; The Hague, The Netherlands; and Karlsruhe, Germany.

A Victorian Romance®, a consumer show begun in February of 1993, focuses on the romantic aspects of that era, including potpourri, afternoon tea, lace and white linens, and collections of all sorts—from hearts to silver teapots and from Crazy quilts to antique fashions. The show features numerous special exhibits, lanes of unique boutiques, and lecture/demonstrations.

Embellishment® is a consumer show that premiered February 24–26, 1995, in Austin, Texas. Sponsored by *BEAD & Button* magazine, the show focused on the infinite varieties of embellishments used in jewelry or on clothing, quilts, and other textile arts. In 1996 it moves to Houston.

Quilts, Inc., Affiliations

The American International Quilt Association (AIQA), the only worldwide, nonprofit quilting association, brings together quilting professionals, quiltmakers, designers, collectors, and enthusiasts. AIQA sponsors one of the most prestigious of the international quilt competitions.

The Alliance for American Quilts is a nonprofit entity and was founded to serve as an umbrella organization under which all elements of the quilt world can unite. Its goal is to achieve a permanent position for quilts as an art form, to preserve the history of quilting in women's lives, and to establish a place for future study and appreciation of quilts.

The Victoria Society is a membership organization for those who are enchanted by the ambiance and elegance of the age of Queen Victoria.

Antique Quilt Styles

If you are new to quilting, it may be difficult for you to recognize the time period in which a particular quilt was made. Added to that problem is the notorious practice among quilters of hoarding fabrics in their stashes and using them years later, creating confusion about when a quilt was made. However, particular styles of quilts, certain fabrics, and popular patterns appear repeatedly, helping to "place" quilts in time.

In reproducing an antique quilt, you can capture the essence of the time in which the quilt was made by using appropriate colors and prints. Colors are usually the easiest elements to reproduce. We can still find fabric of the same Turkey red used in colonial times, and the Nile green used in the 1930s, as well as many reproduction prints from several eras. The secret to making a quilt look antique is knowing which colors, prints, and patterns to use together.

We can categorize most antique quilts into four eras. The quilts in my collection cover all of these time periods.

1840–Civil War

Two styles of quilts were made during this time: utilitarian and fine. Utilitarian pioneer quilts were made of leftover homespun and small calicoes in block settings. The blocks' styles and names reflected events and artifacts of daily life—Log Cabin, Bear's Paw, Churn Dash, Sawtooth Stars—and were used in the modest homes of settlers.

Many fine quilts were made from English chintz purchased to cut apart, appliqué, and embroider with small buttonhole stitches in a method called broderie perse (Persian embroidery). Also appearing at this time were four-block appliqué quilts made to look like medallion coverlets, and the elaborate, time-consuming Baltimore Album quilts. These quilts required fine needle skills and were usually made by upper-class, city women who had both the leisure time and money to make them. Many examples of fine appliqué quilts survive from that time period. Featured fabrics included red and green solids and tone-on-tone prints, as well as large floral chintzes in muted colors. The quilts were usually in block settings and often depicted baskets of fruit, floral bouquets, wreaths, and patriotic themes.

The Civil War saw the demise of many utilitarian quilts. They went to war with the soldiers, were worn out during the long years of battle, and often served as burial shrouds.

1875–1900

Often referred to as 1880s quilts, those made in this time period were distinctive in color. Most of the quilts contained mourning prints and half-mourning prints: black or gray prints with small motifs (probably the remnants of mourning clothes worn for those who had died in the Civil War). Another type of fabric found in quilts from this era was a small seaweed sprig print containing a pink color known as strawberry or double pink. Many off-white shirting prints were used as background colors. Indigo blues, cadet blues, olive greens, browns, Turkey reds, poison greens, clear reds, and yellows all appeared in quilts of this period. The prints ranged from small, two-color calicoes to remnants of larger paisleys, conversation prints, checks, plaids, and other homespun fabrics.

Quilters continued to use simple block patterns, although more difficult patterns began to appear, and patterns with political names became more popular. Block settings became more varied with the use of diagonal sets, alternate blocks, and borders.

1900 (Turn of the Century)

The most popular quilt of the Victorian age was the almost faddish Crazy quilt, which was made of silks, velvets, satins, and scraps of other finery. Crazy quilts were heavily embroidered, not quilted, and were meant to be used as decorative throws.

Also popular at the turn of the century were patriotic quilts made in red, white, and blue.

1930s Quilts

Quilts of the 1930s are currently popular because they were made of grandmothers' aprons and mothers' girlhood dresses, by our mothers and grandmothers. This time period probably has the most easily recognizable quilts. They were almost exclusively pastel with distinctive greens, lavenders, yellows, pinks, and light blues combined with natural muslin or white backgrounds. The simple designs were printed inexpensively with little detailing or shading, and many of the fabrics came from the flour sacks saved by thrifty Depression-era homemakers.

During this time, everyone, it seemed, made a Double Wedding Ring, Dresden Plate, Grandmother's Flower Garden, Baby Blocks, or Sunbonnet Sue. Kits were also available through catalogs, and many well-made and beautiful kit quilts survive today.

About the Book

When That Patchwork Place asked me to write a book about the shop, I decided to feature part of my antique quilt collection. Each of the quilts, collected at various points in my life, has a special place in my heart.

In each section of the book, antique quilts are pictured, and directions for reproducing them are included. In some instances, the sizes vary slightly or the pattern has been modified for ease of construction. Rotary-cutting instructions are provided wherever possible. We've even suggested some options, such as making the Rosebud quilt with Texas yellow roses. General quiltmaking information is provided at the end of the book.

I have also included recipes for dishes that have appeared at almost every Great Expectations function in the past twenty-one years. These recipes have helped us celebrate sales, birthdays, inventories, moving to bigger locations, new show openings, births, marriages—and even diets! (Try the Texas Trifle on page 66.)

This book is about Great Expectations. But it's also about the preservation of our heritage and the love of quilting that we share.

A Family Tradition

Our beds were always covered with handmade, family quilts. When relatives came to visit us, we children slept on what we called Methodist pallets—piles of quilts on the floor. When I was in college, Granny sat my cousin Nancy and me down at the quilting frame at the head of the bed, gave us needles, and said, "Now girls, you learn to take real pretty little stitches because you're going to wake up every morning of your life and have to look at them!"

1930s Five-Pointed String Star

The quilt featured here shares traits with typical 1930s quilts. Small scraps of feed-sack prints, pastels, and clear reds were sewn to a paper foundation and string pieced. However, it is an unusual pattern; most quilts from that era were made using mail-order patterns or patterns printed in newspapers, such as the *Kansas City Star*. The five-pointed star is uncommon, and the stars surrounding the center star make it even more unusual. The pattern is mathematically complex and may have been an original design.

Finished Size: 83½" x 83½"

*Family portrait (opposite), from left to right: Karey Bresenhan, Nancy O'Bryant, Jewel Patterson, and Helen O'Bryant. **1930s Five-Pointed String Star**, 83½" x 83½". Karey loves anything with a Five-Pointed Star—the star that appears in the Texas state flag and in several of her antique quilts.*

Materials: 44"-wide fabric

6 yds. white muslin

5 yds. total assorted scraps or ⅛-yd. pieces of 1930s reproduction prints in pastel colors

1 yd. total assorted scraps of 1930s reproduction solids in light blue, candy pink, lavender, yellow, Nile green, and clear red

8 yds. for backing

¾ yd. for binding

92" x 92" piece of batting

Freezer paper

Typing paper

Cutting

Use the templates on the pullout pattern.

From white muslin, cut:

5 Template #1

10 Template #2

2 pieces, each 37" x 75", for background

4 strips, each 2¼" x 75"*

10 strips, each 2¼" x 42"

*Use fabric trimmed from the sides of the background pieces.

From assorted scraps of prints and solid fabrics, cut:

1"- to 3"-wide strips for string piecing

5 squares, each 2" x 2"

From freezer paper, cut:

5 Template #3

From typing paper, cut:

50 Template #4

Piecing the Large Star

1. Trim one side of each of the 2" x 2" assorted print squares to create 5-sided pieces. Place one on the shiny side of a large freezer-paper star point (piece #3). Lightly press the piece *with the tip of your iron only* to make the fabric adhere to the paper.

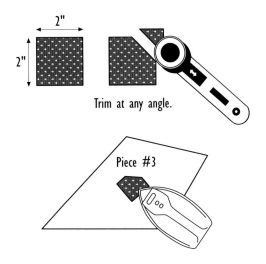

4. Add pieces until fabric extends at least ¼" beyond the paper template on all sides. (Once the pieces at the sides extend far enough, add strips roughly parallel to each other at each end until the points are covered.) Trim ¼" from the edge of the freezer paper on all sides.

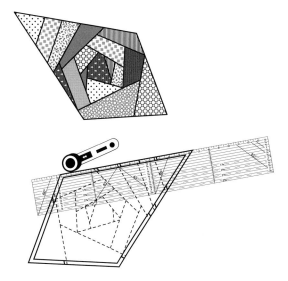

2. Add a print or solid strip of fabric to the first piece, right sides together, lining up the edges. Sew ¼" from the edge of the fabric pieces. Fold the strip open and press.

3. Continue adding pieces clockwise around the center piece as shown. Trim at the seam line as each new piece is added.

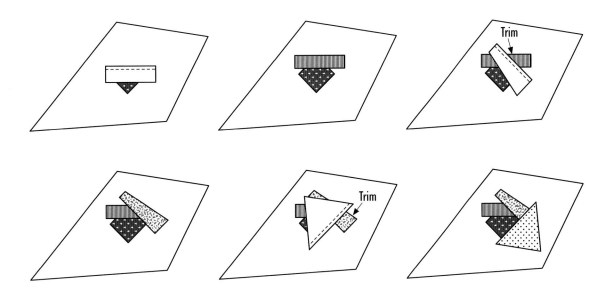

Mexican Cornbread

Great with chili or a pot of pinto beans!

1½ Tablespoons salad oil or bacon
      drippings
¼ cup flour
1 cup yellow cornmeal
1 teaspoon salt
½ teaspoon soda
2 eggs
¾ cup milk
1 small can cream-style corn
2 small jalapeño peppers, chopped, with
      seeds removed
½ lb. sharp cheddar cheese, grated

   Preheat oven to 425° F. Put oil or bacon drippings in a 9" x 13" baking dish and place in oven to heat while mixing the other ingredients. Mix together flour, cornmeal, salt, and soda. Add eggs and stir well. Blend in milk gradually. Add the corn, peppers, and all but 1 cup of the cheddar cheese; stir well.

   Pour batter into pan when oil is smoking hot. Top with remaining cheese. Bake for 25 minutes. Serves 4 generously or 2 with leftovers. Reheat in the microwave or wrap in foil and heat in oven.

5. Sew together 2 star points, beginning and ending the stitching ¼" from the corners.

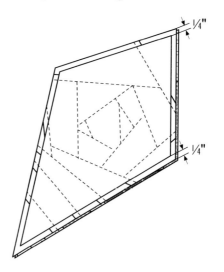

6. Add another point to the pair in the same manner. Sew the 2 remaining points together and sew them to the set of 3 points, matching seams at the center of the star.

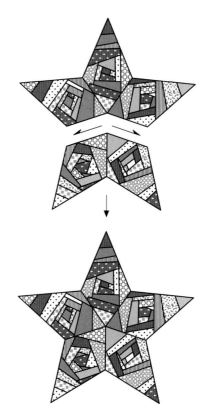

Piecing the Small Stars

1. String-piece the small stars, using the 50 typing-paper star points (piece #4). Begin with a strip across the middle of a paper star-point foundation. Place another strip on the first with right sides together. Sew, flip, trim, and press until the paper is covered with strips that extend ¼" or more beyond the edges of the template. Trim the fabric edges ¼" away from the paper edge to allow for seams.

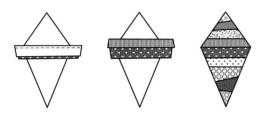

2. Sew the points together as for the large star.

Make 10 small stars.

Looking Back...

String piecing, common in the 1920s and 1930s, was an effective way to avoid waste by using small scraps of fabric. Often, pieces were sewn to a foundation of old letters, newspapers, or other lightweight paper. Newspaper was used for large pieces, and long strips of string piecing were often one newspaper column wide. Instead of having to measure, the quilter simply cut the paper into columns and covered the strips. The border of this quilt may have been done this way. Today, we aren't quite so frugal (and newspaper is so messy), so we use typing paper and freezer paper instead.

Assembling the Quilt Top

1. Sew a piece #1 to the center large star. Sew from the seam intersection of the star points to the ends of the points as shown. Add the 4 remaining #1 pieces around the large star. Gently remove the freezer paper from the back of the large star.

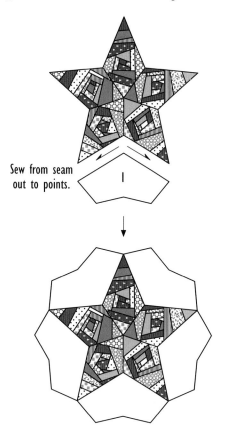

Sew from seam out to points.

2. Sew a piece #2 diamond to the right side of each small star. Sew from one star point to the other. To pivot at the side point of the diamond, leave the needle in the fabric, lift the presser foot, turn the work slightly, lower the presser foot, and continue sewing.

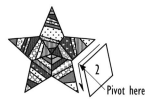

Pivot here

3. Sew the small star/diamond sets together to form a ring. Sew from the point of the diamond at the inner edge of the ring to the outer point as shown, pivoting at the seam intersection.

Pivot here

4. Pin the small star/diamond circle to the center star unit, matching the large star points with the diamond points. Sew the star/diamond circle and the center unit together, pivoting at the center of each piece #1 and at the large star points. Clip at the center point of piece #1 if necessary.

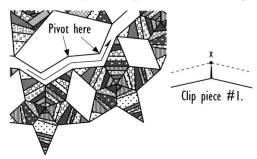

Pivot here

Clip piece #1.

5. Sew together the 2 muslin 37" x 75" background pieces lengthwise, using a ¼"-wide seam allowance; press the seam open. Fold the background in half as shown and lightly press the fold. The center of the background should be where the fold crosses the seam; measure to be sure.

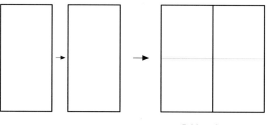

Fold and press.

6. Match the center of the star "medallion" to the center of the background. Orient the large star as shown in the quilt photo and diagram on pages 11 and 12. Turn under the edges of the star medallion ¼", using the edges of the paper foundations to fold against for a sharp crease. Pin or baste the entire medallion in place and appliqué it to the background.

7. On the back side of the quilt top, trim away the fabric behind the center medallion, leaving a ¼"-wide seam allowance. Gently remove the paper foundations from the small stars.

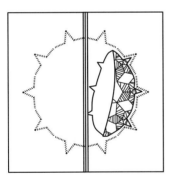

8. Trim the background to measure 71" x 71".

Assembling the Border

1. String-piece strips of the assorted prints onto 17 sheets of typing paper in the same

manner as for the star points. Trim the edges even with the edges of the paper.

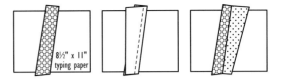

2. Use a rotary ruler and cutter to measure and cut 4 strips, each 2" wide, from each sheet of string-pieced typing paper.

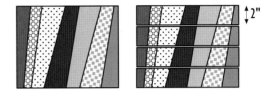

3. Sew the string-pieced strips together end to end to make 8 strips, each 88" long.

4. Sew the 2¼"-wide strips of muslin together end to end and trim to make 8 strips, each 88" long. Sew an 88"-long muslin strip to each 88"-long string-pieced strip. Sew pairs together as shown to make the double borders as shown below.

5. Referring to the information on "Borders with Mitered Corners" on pages 90–91, sew double border strips to the top, bottom, and sides of the quilt, stopping ¼" from the corners. Then, miter the corners of the borders.

Finishing

Refer to pages 91–95 for information on finishing your quilt.

1. Mark the quilt top with the ¾"-wide grid and the feather designs on the pullout pattern, or mark as desired.

2. Layer the quilt top with batting and backing.

3. Baste, quilt, and bind.

4. Label your Five-Pointed String Star quilt.

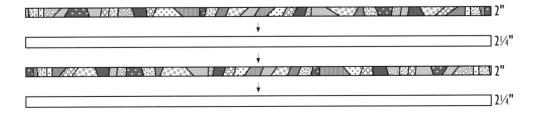

The Run for Office

This beautiful Stars and Stripes quilt came into my life years after my run for the Texas State Legislature in 1974. But it represents to me many ideas related to that time, and particularly the notion that women can do anything. Since I couldn't get funding for my legislative campaign any other way, I raised about $40,000 buying quilts and antiques and selling them at shows in my friends' homes. I learned a lot about life and quilts during that time. One of those lessons was that people relate to quilts no matter what their ages, incomes, or political persuasions.

Stars and Stripes

This quilt is tied rather than quilted—a common technique for a quilt meant to be used daily as a bedcover. Many such utilitarian quilts did not survive the rigors of everyday wear. The backing of the original quilt is an 1890s shirting-type fabric. The original quilt has an "extra" row of Drunkard's Path units, probably to make it a certain size. You may wish to omit that row to keep the design symmetrical.

Finished Size: 73½" x 66½"
Star Block Size: 7" x 14" • Drunkard's Path Block Size: 14" x 14"

***Stars and Stripes** by unknown quilter, circa 1900, 73½" x 66½". Karey collected this patriotic piece to remind her of her run for the Texas State Legislature.*

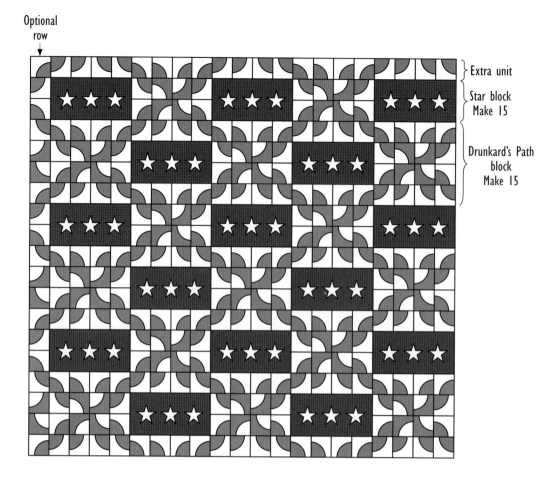

Optional row

Extra unit

Star block
Make 15

Drunkard's Path block
Make 15

Materials: 44"-wide fabric

1⅝ yds. blue solid
4 yds. white solid
3½ yds. red solid
4½ yds. for backing
⅝ yd. for binding
76" x 82" piece of batting
Perle cotton or embroidery floss to tie quilt
Optional: You may wish to use paper-backed
    fusible web to "appliqué" the stars, then
    buttonhole-stitch around each one.

Cutting

Use the templates on the pullout pattern.
From blue solid fabric, cut:
    8 strips, each 7½" x 42". Crosscut into
        15 rectangles, each 7½" x 14½".
From white solid fabric, cut:
    213 Template A
    66 Template B
    45 stars

From red solid fabric, cut:
    66 Template A
    213 Template B

Assembling the Blocks

1. Referring to the appliqué information beginning on page 85, appliqué 3 white stars to each blue rectangle.

2. To construct the following Drunkard's Path units, mark the curved edges of the block pieces at the center in the seam allowances for easier matching. Pin piece A and piece B together along the curved edge, matching the center marks. Sew the pieces together carefully, easing as necessary.

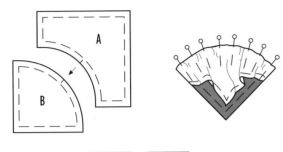

Unit 1
Make 66   Unit 2
Make 213

3. Arrange the Drunkard's Path units in rows as shown in the diagram. Sew the units together, pressing the seams in rows 1 and 3 in one direction and the seams in rows 2 and 4 in the other direction.

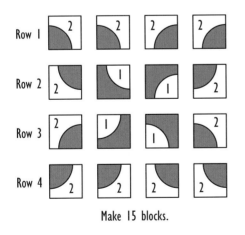

Row 1

Row 2

Row 3

Row 4

Make 15 blocks.

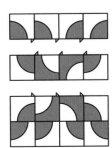

4. Sew together 4 of Unit 2 as shown to make strips for the tops of rows 1, 3, and 5, and the bottoms of rows 2 and 4.

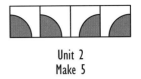

Unit 2
Make 5

5. If you want to add the extra row of Drunkard's Path blocks that appears on the left side in the original quilt, sew together the units shown below.

Assembling the Quilt Top

1. Arrange the strips with the appliquéd star blocks and the Drunkard's Path blocks in vertical rows, referring to the quilt plan for placement.

2. Sew the blocks together into rows, then sew the vertical rows together.

Finishing

Refer to pages 91–95 for information on finishing your quilt.

1. Layer the quilt top with batting and backing.

2. Using the perle cotton or embroidery floss and referring to the diagram on page 20, tie the quilt at the centers of the Drunkard's Path blocks and at block intersections. (See page 93 for information on tying quilts.)

3. Label your Stars and Stripes quilt.

Opening Great Expectations

Two weeks after my unsuccessful run for the Texas legislature, my mother-in-law, Mary Kelly Bresenhan, and I found an enormous space in Houston for our antique shop. Our first problem was that we lacked the money to fill our antique shop with antiques. We decided to hang my family quilts everywhere because they could hide some of the empty shop space very well. Our customers were so enthusiastic about the quilts, we began to buy and sell antique quilts.

Rosebud Appliqué

Reproduction designed by Rachael Lambrecht.

Finished Size: 77½" x 94¼" • **Block Size: 10½" x 10½"**

Rosebud Appliqué *by unknown quilter, 1930s kit, 77½" x 94¼". This quilt was a "show" quilt
and was finely quilted, embroidered, and appliquéd.*

Rosebud Appliqué 24

Materials: 44"-wide fabric

6 yds. white solid for background and borders

1⅝ yds. blue solid for sashing and binding

1¼ yds. green solid for leaves

1¾ yds. brown solid for stems

⅛ yd. dark rose solid for flower centers

¼ yd. medium rose solid for inner flower petals

¼ yd. light rose solid for outer flower petals

6 yds. white for backing

84" x 100" piece of batting

Paper-backed fusible web

Embroidery floss in red, brown, 3 shades of rose, and green

NOTE: This pattern is reproduced using paper-backed fusible web to secure the appliqués. For ease in using that method, the appliqué patterns given are the reverse of the shapes on the quilt.

Cutting

Use the templates on the pullout pattern. Refer to the instructions for "Fusible Appliqué" on pages 87–88, to cut the appliqué pieces for the blocks and borders.

From white solid fabric, cut:
 2 squares, each 10⅛" x 10⅛". Crosscut once diagonally for corner triangles.
 2 squares, each 18¼" x 18¼". Crosscut twice diagonally for side setting triangles.
 8 squares, each 11" x 11", for blocks
 4 squares, each 20½" x 20½", for border corners
 2 strips, each 20½" x 35½", for borders
 2 strips, each 20½" x 52¼", for borders

From blue solid fabric, cut:
 15 strips, each 1¾" x 42"

From green solid fabric, cut:
 40 Template #5
 136 Template #6
 68 Template #7

From brown solid fabric, cut:
 6 Template #1
 10 Template #8
 4 Template #9

From dark rose solid fabric, cut:
 40 Template #2

From medium rose solid fabric, cut:
 40 Template #3

From light rose solid fabric, cut:
 40 Template #4

Appliquéing Blocks and Borders

1. Referring to the full-size design on the pull-out pattern, fuse the required pieces to the background blocks in numerical order.

2. Buttonhole-stitch around each appliqué piece with matching embroidery floss. Using red floss, satin-stitch thorns along the stems.

Buttonhole Stitch   Satin Stitch

When stitching on a narrow piece of fabric, stagger stitches as shown below:

Rachael's Small Wall Hanging

Rachael Lambrecht, designer of the reproduction pattern,
appliquéd the block motif onto four blocks straight up rather
than diagonally, made the roses yellow for the state of Texas,
and added 1"-wide sashing and borders.

3. Referring to the full-size design on the pullout pattern and the quilt plan on page 24, fuse the appliqué motifs to the corner blocks and border strips. Leave the ends of the vines free where they will overlap the border seams.

   NOTE: Leaves that are shaded on the appliqué patterns overlap the border seams and are fused onto the quilt after assembly is completed.

4. Buttonhole-stitch around each appliqué piece with matching embroidery floss. Add red satin-stitched thorns.

Assembling the Quilt Top

1. Sew the 1¼"-wide sashing strips end to end and crosscut into:
   12 pieces, each 1¾" x 11"
   2 pieces, each 1¾" x 13½"
   2 pieces, each 1¾" x 35½"
   1 piece, 1¾" x 47½"
   2 pieces, each 1¾" x 37"
   4 pieces, each 1¾" x 20½"
   2 pieces, each 1¾" x 94¾"

2. Arrange the appliquéd blocks, alternate blocks, sashing, and side and corner setting triangles into rows as shown.

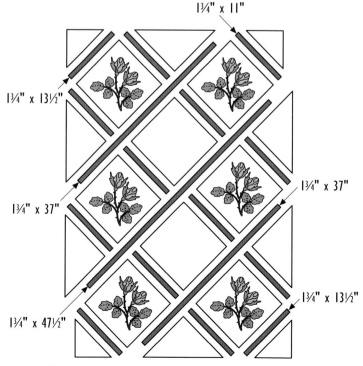

3. Sew the blocks together in diagonal rows, pressing the seams toward the sashing. Sew the rows together to complete the center of the quilt top.

Adding the Borders

1. Sew sashing strips to the top and bottom borders as shown and add them to the quilt top.

← 1¾" x 35½"

Looking Back...

The Rosebud quilt was one of many made from kits during the 1930s. Since quilt shops didn't exist then, ordering a kit from a catalog was the only way most women could make a planned and coordinated quilt. The kits included quality fabrics, and the finished products were considered "best" quilts as opposed to the utility quilts made from feed sacks and other scraps. Quilters usually displayed their best quilting, embroidery, and appliqué in these quilts.

2. Sew together the border corner squares, sashing strips, side border strips, and side sashing strips as shown. Add the borders to the sides of the quilt, matching border seams at the top and bottom as shown below right.

3. Fuse the appliqué pieces (leaves) that overlap the border corner seams to the quilt top. Outline them with buttonhole stitches.

4. Using Templates #10 and #11, lightly trace scallops along the edges of the quilt.

Finishing

Refer to pages 91–95 for information on finishing your quilt.

1. Mark the quilt top with quilting designs as desired.

2. Layer the quilt top with backing and batting.

3. Baste and quilt.

4. Trim the edges of the quilt along the marked scallop lines.

5. Make and bind the quilt with bias binding.

6. Label your Rosebud Appliqué quilt.

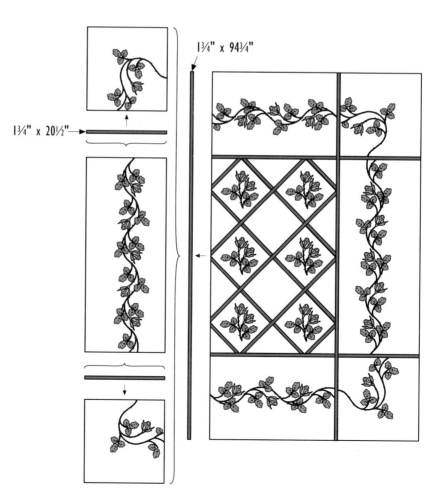

1¾" x 94¾"

1¾" x 20½"

Chocolate "Sheath" Cake

At least three decades of Texas brides have faithfully passed along this recipe for a "Sheath" cake—surely an error at some point, since this is a classic *sheet* cake. A chocoholic's dream cake—thick, moist, and fudge-y!

1 stick butter
½ cup oil
4 Tablespoons cocoa
1 cup water
2 cups unsifted all-purpose flour
1 teaspoon soda
2 cups sugar
½ cup sour milk*
2 eggs, beaten
1 teaspoon vanilla

*Buttermilk is fine, or put 1½ teaspoons vinegar in ½ cup sweet milk to sour it.

Preheat oven to 350° F. Mix butter, oil, cocoa, and water in a saucepan. Heat and stir until mixed. Combine flour, soda, sugar, milk, eggs, and vanilla in a large bowl. Pour in cocoa mixture and stir well. Pour batter into a greased 12" x 18" pan. Bake 20 to 25 minutes or until a pick inserted in center comes out clean. Prepare icing while cake is baking.

Chocolate Icing

1 stick butter
4 Tablespooons cocoa
6 Tablespoons milk
1 lb. powdered sugar
1 teaspoon vanilla
1 cup pecans

Combine butter, cocoa, and milk in saucepan. Heat until bubbles form around the edge and mixture turns glossy. Remove from heat, add powdered sugar, vanilla, and pecans. Beat. Ice cake while it is still warm.

International

Quilt Festival

Great Expectations was already thriving by the end of its first year. So I threw a "Thank-you to Houston" party—the beginning of International Quilt Festival—right there in the shop with a quilt exhibit and lectures on quilt dating and conservation. Would you believe it? Several thousand people lined up across the parking lot all the way to the street just to come in. The next year, my mother, Jewel Pearce Patterson, a full-time school librarian and lifelong quilter, started teaching quilting classes in the evenings and on weekends. By May, Mother and I had started the Quilt Guild of Greater Houston, which met at the shop for its first year. Today, the Quilt Guild has 400 members. "Festival" draws at least 50,000 people each fall and is held in the huge George R. Brown Convention Center in Houston.

Prairie Flower

The Prairie Flower quilt in my collection is not an appliqué quilt. Rather, each motif is pieced into a muslin background with precise leaves, rounded flowers, and tiny stems. Each circle of muslin is then pieced into the print background. It is hard to imagine anyone attempting to piece such an intricate pattern, especially since the pattern is so similar to appliqué patterns from the same era. Lisa DeBee Schiller, appliqué and Baltimore Album teacher at Great Expectations, designed and translated the pattern to appliqué.

This hand-pieced quilt sold almost immediately at the first Quilt Festival. Several years later, I had the opportunity to buy the quilt back.

Finished Size: 78" x 83" • Block Size: 22" x 22"

Quilt Festival (opposite)—an overview of Quilt Festival in the George R. Brown Convention Center in Houston.
Prairie Flower *by unknown quilter, circa 1870–75, 78" x 83". (Quilts, Inc., Corporate Collection)*

31

Materials: 44"-wide fabric

3¼ yds. muslin for appliquéd circles
1½ yds. poison green for leaves and vases
½ yd. green solid for bias stems
½ yd. double pink for light part of flowers
½ yd. deep red for flowers
⅛ yd. gold for centers of flowers
7¾ yds. peach print for background blocks
8¼ yds. for backing
1 yd. red solid for bias binding
96" x 96" piece of batting
Bias bars
Freezer paper

Cutting

Make templates using the half-block diagram on the pullout pattern. Refer to "Needle-Turn Appliqué" on page 86 to prepare all appliqué shapes except pieces #8 and #10. Refer to "Freezer-Paper Appliqué" on pages 85–86 to prepare pieces #8 and #10.

From muslin, cut:
    9 squares, each 22" x 22"
From poison green fabric, cut:
    27 Template #4
    27 Template #4 reversed
    9 Template #11
    27 Template #3
    153 Template #8
    9 Template #9
    18 Template #10
From green solid fabric, cut:
    9 bias strips, each 1½" x 36"
From double pink fabric, cut:
    27 Template #1
    9 Template #5
From deep red fabric, cut:
    27 Template #2
    9 Template #6
From gold fabric, cut:
    9 Template #7
From peach print, cut:
    9 squares, each 26½" x 26½"
    2 strips, each 3" x 78½"
From freezer paper, cut:
    153 Template #8
    18 Template #10

Assembling the Blocks

1. Using the half-block diagram on the pull-out pattern, trace placement lines for the appliqué pieces onto the muslin background squares.
2. Referring to "Making Bias Stems" on page 88, prepare 9 bias stems, each 27" long, and 9 short stems, each 3" long, from the green bias strips.
3. Pin or baste the appliqué pieces to the background circles. Appliqué the bias stem pieces, then the flowers, buds, and leaves in numerical order.
4. Use the pullout pattern to trace the flattened circle shape surrounding the Prairie Flower motif onto each of the 26½" x 26½" peach-print background blocks. Fold the block in quarters to find the center. Center the block over the pattern and trace half of the flattened circle onto the block. Reverse the pattern and trace the other half.

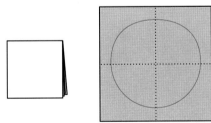

5. Cut away the fabric inside the flattened circle outline on the peach-print blocks, leaving a ¼"-wide seam allowance. Carefully clip almost to the seam line at intervals around the circle.

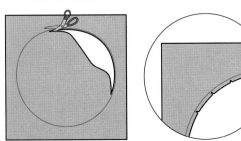

6. Center the background block over the appliquéd block. Pin or baste the blocks together, then turn the seam allowance of the peach fabric under, just beyond the traced seam line, as you appliqué it to the muslin block.

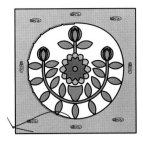

7. Trim muslin from the back after the appliqué is finished.

Assembling the Quilt Top

1. Arrange the blocks side by side in 3 rows of 3, with the blocks in the outer rows pointing toward the center as shown.
2. Sew the 3" x 78½" border strips to the top and bottom of the quilt.

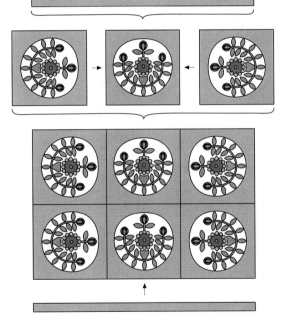

Finishing

Refer to pages 91–95 for information on finishing your quilt.

1. Mark the quilt top for quilting. The Prairie Flower motifs were echo quilted, and the background was quilted with a ½" grid on the diagonal.
2. Layer the quilt top with backing and batting.
3. Baste, quilt, and bind.
4. Label your Prairie Flower quilt.

International
Quilt Market

I used to spend hours on Sunday morning talking to my friend Florence Zentner, founder of The Quiltworks, a division of Knit-Kits, Inc. We'd talk about customers being unable to find yellow fabrics and about store owners having no place to get together to trade information. Florence convinced me it was up to me to try my hand at putting on an industry-wide trade show where retailers could buy supplies for their shops. Today, we call it the International Quilt Market. I know that Market has truly helped quilters. If it has done nothing else, it has helped the customer find yellow!

Contained Crazy Quilt

This early, restrained, and unadorned block-style Crazy quilt is most likely an example of recycling unused blocks. Because the fabric is all from the same era—therefore similar in color and tone—the blocks seem related and unified.

Finished Size: 70" x 79"

The Quintessential Quilt Shop (opposite)—Great Expectations—at Quilt Festival. Photo by Blair Pittman. **Contained Crazy Quilt** *by unknown quilter, circa 1870, 70" x 79". This beautiful Sampler quilt was purchased at International Quilt Market. (Quilts, Inc., Corporate Collection)*

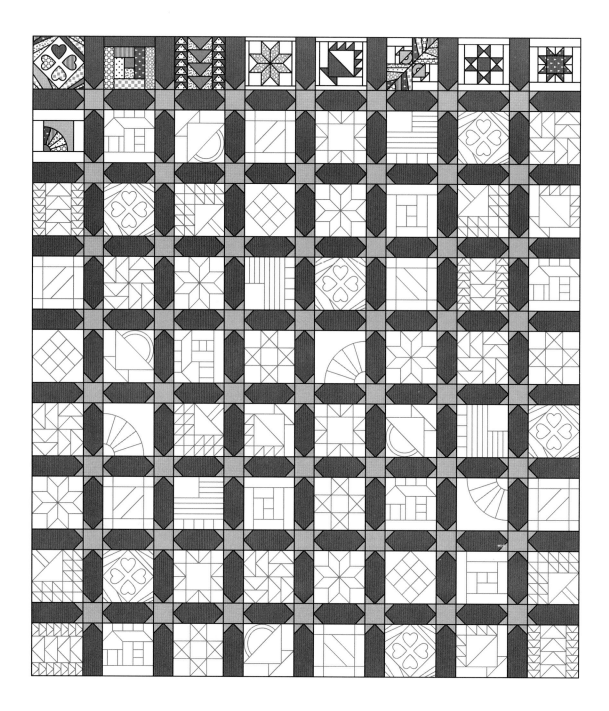

Materials: 44"-wide fabric

2¼ yds. red print for sashing

1¾ yds. yellow for stars in sashing

4 yds. assorted scraps, fat quarters, or ⅛-yd. pieces in 1880s style and color, such as blacks, madder reds, Dijon mustards, double pinks, colonial blues, conversation prints, and shirtings

5 yds. for backing

⅝ yd. red for binding

75" x 86" piece of batting

Sashing

Cutting

From red print, cut:

22 strips, each 3" x 42". Crosscut into 127 strips, each 3" x 7".

From yellow fabric, cut:

19 strips, each 1¾" x 42". Crosscut into 448 squares, each 1¾" x 1¾".

4 strips, each 3" x 42". Crosscut into 56 squares, each 3" x 3".

Assembling the Sashing

1. To make the star sashing, draw a diagonal line from corner to corner on the wrong side of each of the yellow squares.

2. Place a yellow square on a corner of a sashing strip with right sides together and sew on the drawn line.

3. Trim away the corner, leaving a ¼"-wide seam allowance. Fold the yellow triangle open and press.

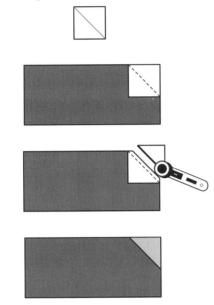

4. Add another square to the adjacent corner in the same way for the sashing units on the ends of the rows. Add squares to all 4 corners for the other sashing units.

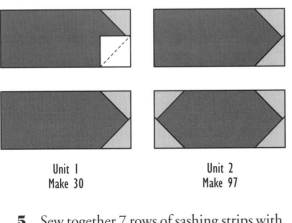

Unit 1
Make 30

Unit 2
Make 97

5. Sew together 7 rows of sashing strips with yellow squares as shown below.

Vertical Sashing Strip
Make 7

NOTE: This is not a formally planned quilt. It appears that the maker used unmatched blocks and scraps from her collection, cutting down or adding to them as needed to make them all measure 7" x 7" for a 6½" x 6½" finished size. There are several common types of blocks used in the original quilt. We are providing instructions for some of these blocks: Log Cabin, Flying Geese, Checkerboard, Star, Basket, Grandmother's Fan, and the appliquéd hearts. You can add blocks from your collection and piece them together, Crazy-quilt style.

Log Cabin

Block Size: 6½" x 6½"

The Log Cabin block appears in several places in the quilt, as part or all of a block. Make as many Log Cabin blocks as you would like to use in the quilt. The original quilt contains eight Log Cabin blocks in various sizes and colorations. Use the following information to make one Log Cabin block.

Cutting

From each of 3 light prints, cut:
2 strips, each 1¾" x 7"

From each of 3 dark prints, cut:
2 strips each 1¾" x 7"

From red solid fabric, cut:
1 square, 1¼" x 1¼"

Assembling the Block

1. Place the red square on the end of a light strip, right sides together. Sew the piece to the strip, using a ¼"-wide seam.
2. Trim the strip even with the square and press open.

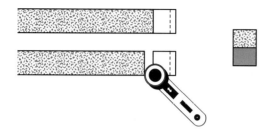

3. Turn the square/strip unit so that the light square is at the top. Place a light strip on top, right sides together. Sew the strip to the unit, using a ¼"-wide seam allowance. Press and trim the strip.
4. Add a dark strip to the next side. Continue adding strips clockwise.

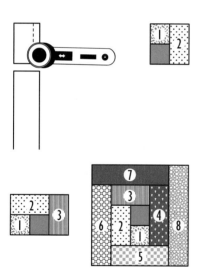

Flying Geese

Block Size: 6½" x 6½"

In the original quilt, a block with Flying Geese has a center row of brown and pink geese with two outer rows of yellow and black geese. Use the following information to make one Flying Geese block.

Cutting

From ⅛ yd. of brown fabric, cut:
4 rectangles, each 2⅛" x 3½"
From ⅛ yd. of pink fabric, cut:
8 squares, each 2⅛" x 2⅛"
From ⅛ yd. of yellow print, cut:
14 rectangles, each 1½" x 2½"
From ⅛ yd. of black print, cut:
28 squares, each 1½" x 1½"
From a scrap of any color fabric, cut:
1 strip, 1" x 7"

Assembling the Block

1. On the wrong side of each of the pink and black print squares, lightly mark a straight line from corner to corner with a sharp pencil.
2. Place a pink square on one end of a brown rectangle, right sides together. Sew on the drawn line and trim ¼" away from the stitching as shown. Fold open and press. Repeat with another pink square at the other end of the brown rectangle.

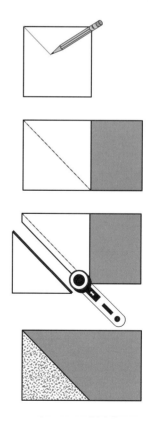

3. Sew the 4 flying-geese units together into a strip as shown.

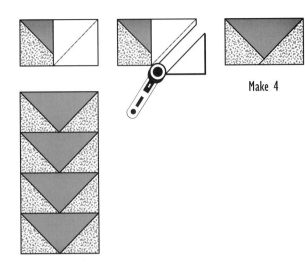

Make 4

4. Use the same method to sew the black squares and the yellow rectangles together. Make 14 flying-geese units.

5. Sew the yellow and black flying-geese units together into 2 strips of 7.

6. Sew a strip of yellow and black geese to each side of the strip of pink and brown geese.

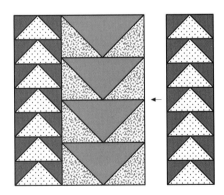

Checkerboard Blocks

Block Size: 6½" x 6½"

All of the following combinations of checkerboard blocks appear in the original quilt, including Four Patches, Ninepatches, and checkerboards with 16 and 25 squares. Each was used as part of a block and enlarged with strips around it to increase the block size to 6½".

FOUR PATCH AND 16 PATCH

1. Cut a light strip and a dark strip, each 1½" x 42".

2. Sew the strips together lengthwise and crosscut into 1½"-wide segments.

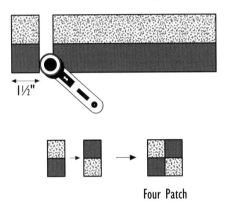

1½"

Four Patch

3. Sew 2 segments together to make a Four Patch block. Sew 4 units together to make a 16-patch block.

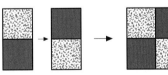

Four Patch

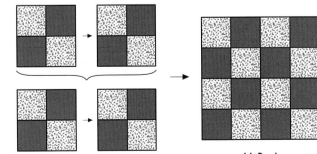

16 Patch

Ninepatch

1. Cut 3 light strips and 3 dark strips, each 1½" x 42".
2. Sew together 2 sets of strips: 1 set with 2 light strips and 1 dark strip, and 1 set with 1 light strip and 2 dark strips.
3. Crosscut the strip sets into 1½"-wide segments. Sew together segments as shown to complete the Ninepatch block.

25 Patch

1. Cut 5 light strips and 5 dark strips, each 1½" x 42". Sew together 2 sets of 5 strips, alternating light and dark as shown.
2. Crosscut the sets into 1½"-wide segments. Arrange the segments as shown and sew them together into rows.
3. Sew the rows together to complete the 25-patch block.

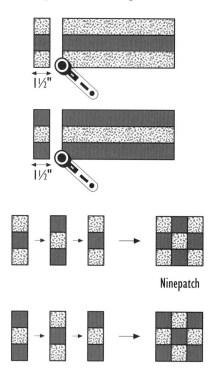

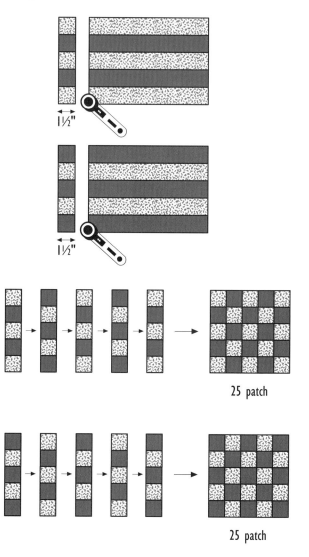

Star Blocks

Several different kinds of stars appear in this quilt, including Ohio Stars, Variable Stars, and Eight-Pointed Stars. All of the stars in the quilt are 4" to 5" square and were enlarged by adding strips.

OHIO STAR

Block Size: 4½" x 4½"

Cutting

From ⅛ yd. of light background fabric, cut:
  1 strip, 2" x 8". Crosscut into 4 squares, each 2" x 2".
  2 squares, each 2¾" x 2¾". Crosscut twice diagonally into 8 triangles.

From ⅛ yd. of contrasting fabric, cut:
  1 square, 2" x 2"
  2 squares, each 2¾" x 2¾". Crosscut twice diagonally into 8 triangles.

Assembling the Block

1. Sew together light and dark triangles as shown to make quarter-square triangles.

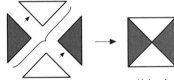

Make 4

2. Arrange the quarter-square triangles with the light and dark squares and sew them together in rows.

3. Sew the rows together to complete the Ohio Star block.

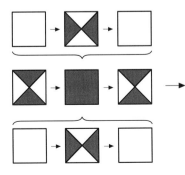

Ohio Star

VARIABLE STAR

Block Size: 4" x 4"

Cutting

From ⅛ yd. of background fabric, cut:
  4 squares, each 1½" x 1½"
  1 strip, 1⅞" x 8". Crosscut into 4 squares, each 1⅞" x 1⅞"; crosscut once diagonally.

From ⅛ yd. of contrasting fabric, cut:
  1 strip, 1⅞" x 10". Crosscut into 4 squares, each 1⅞" x 1⅞"; crosscut once diagonally.
  1 square, 2½" x 2½"

Assembling the Block

1. Sew together light and dark triangles to make half-square triangles.

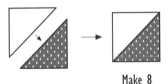

Make 8

2. Arrange the half-square triangles and light and dark squares and sew them together as shown to complete the Variable Star block.

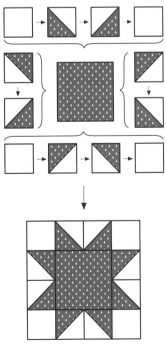

Variable Star

EIGHT-POINTED STAR

Block Size: 5⅛" x 5⅛"

Cutting

From ⅛ yd. of background fabric, cut:
  4 squares, each 2" x 2"
  1 square, 3⅜" x 3⅜". Crosscut twice
  diagonally for side triangles.
From ⅛ yd. of contrasting fabric, cut:
  8 Template #1

Assembling the Block

1. Sew a piece #1 to a side triangle. Begin stitching ¼" from the edge of the triangle and sew all the way to the outer edge.

2. Add another piece #1 to the same side triangle.

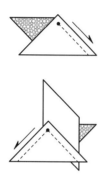

3. Sew the piece #1 pieces together, stitching from the intersection of the 2 previous seams to the outer edge.

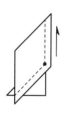

Make 4

4. Sew a square of background fabric to the left side of the unit. Begin stitching ¼" from the edge of piece #1 as shown and continue to the outer edge.

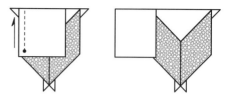

5. Sew together pairs of units to make half stars. Stitch from the ¼" seam line to each outer edge.

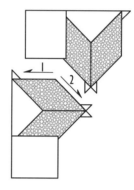

6. Sew together half stars, pinning and stitching carefully first from seam intersections to outer edges, then from seam intersection to seam intersection across the center.

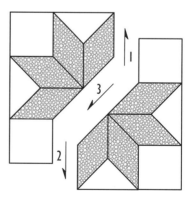

Basket Blocks

Two different Basket blocks appear in this quilt: a Cake Stand block and a Postage Stamp Basket block.

CAKE STAND

Block Size: 5" x 5"

Cutting

From ¼ yd. of light background fabric, cut:

1 strip, 1⅞" x 6". Crosscut into 3 squares, each 1⅞" x 1⅞"; crosscut each square once diagonally.

1 square, 3⅞" x 3⅞". Crosscut once diagonally.

1 strip, 1½" x 10". Crosscut into 2 rectangles, each 1½" x 3½", and 1 square, 1½" x 1½".

1 square, 2⅞" x 2⅞". Crosscut once diagonally.

From ⅛ yd. of contrasting fabric, cut:

1 strip, 1⅞" x 10". Crosscut into 4 squares, each 1⅞". Cut squares once diagonally.

1 square, 3⅞" x 3⅞". Cut once diagonally.

Assembling the Block

1. Sew together the background and basket triangles to make half-square triangle units.

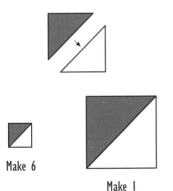

Make 6

Make 1

2. Arrange the half-square triangle units and the remaining pieces and sew them to-

gether as shown to complete the Cake Stand block.

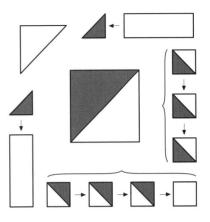

POSTAGE STAMP BASKET

Block Size: 2" x 2"
Cutting (for 2 blocks)

From light background fabric, cut:

1 square, 2⅜" x 2⅜". Cut once diagonally.

2 squares, each 1⅞" x 1⅞". Cut once diagonally.

1 strip, 1" x 6". Crosscut into 4 rectangles, each 1" x 1½".

From a scrap of contrasting fabric, cut:

1 square, 2⅜" x 2⅜". Cut once diagonally.

2 squares, each 1⅜" x 1⅜". Cut once diagonally.

1 bias strip, 1½" x 6", for handle

Assembling the Block

1. Fold the bias strip in half lengthwise, wrong sides together. Sew along the length of the strip ¼" from the edge. Cut the strip in half for 2 basket handles.

2. Fold under the seam allowance of the bias strip just beyond the stitching and press.

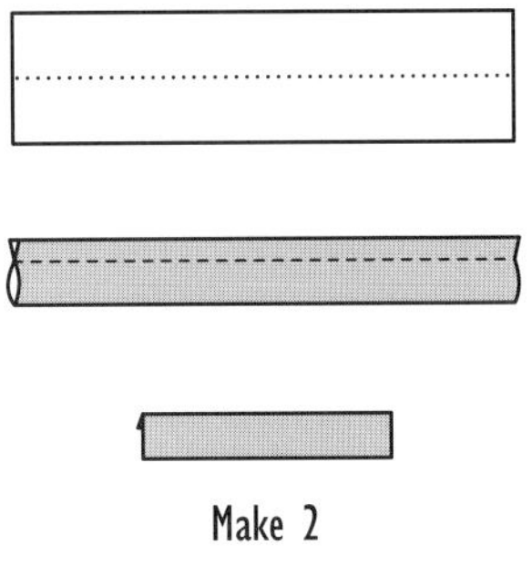

Make 2

3. Pin the bias basket handle to the large background triangle and appliqué it in place, leaving ¼" between the handle and the sides of the triangle for seam allowances.

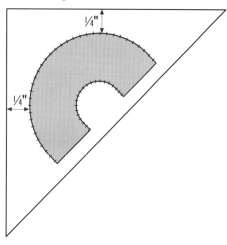

4. Sew together the 2 large triangles.

5. Sew a small triangle to one end of each rectangle.

6. Sew the pieces together as shown to complete the Postage Stamp Basket block.

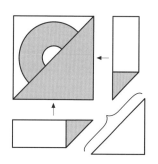

7. Join blocks, adding strips as necessary to make a 7" block. (See Note on page 45.)

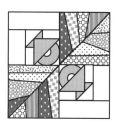

Grandmother's Fan

Block Size: 3½" x 3½"

This pattern appears in the quilt as a quarter, half, and full circle (Dresden Plate).

Cutting

Use the templates on the pullout pattern.
From scraps of assorted prints, cut:
    5 Template #2 for each quarter-circle fan desired
    1 Template #4 for center of fan
From a scrap of background fabric, cut:
    1 Template #3 for each quarter-circle fan

Assembling the Block

1. Sew #2 pieces together to make a quarter-circle fan. Sew together quarter-circle fans as desired to make half circles and full circles.

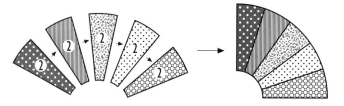

2. Appliqué the fan center, piece #4, to the corner of the fan.

3. Sew the fan to the background, piece #3, easing as necessary.

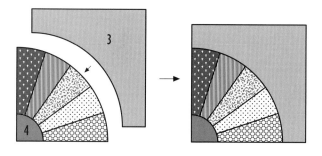

NOTE: Sew quarter-circle fans together to make half circles and full circles as desired.

Appliquéd Blocks

Block Size: 4½" x 4½"

In addition to the pieced blocks, there are a few appliquéd blocks. The only recognizable pattern, however, is a group of 4 hearts.

Cutting

Refer to "Freezer-Paper Appliqué" on pages 85–86 to prepare templates from the pullout pattern.

From assorted scraps, cut:
   4 Template #5
From ⅛ yd. of background fabric, cut:
   1 square, 5" x 5"

Assembling the Block

1. Using the freezer-paper appliqué method, appliqué each heart to the square of background fabric.

2. See the note above left to finish the Heart block.

NOTE: *Making 7" Blocks*

Most of the blocks in this quilt are pieced together from parts of blocks and/or have strips added around the sides to bring them to 7" x 7". Capture the spontaneous feel of the original quilt by randomly adding strips and pieces to blocks that are smaller than the desired size. Cut fabric into strips of various widths from ¾" to 3". Add strips to some or all sides. Sew some strips diagonally for a Crazy-quilt look. Keep adding strips until the block measures more than 7" all around, then trim to 7" x 7". Make 72 blocks.

Assembling the Quilt Top

1. Trim all blocks to 7" x 7". Do not worry about grain line or the parts of the block you are losing. You can recycle the trimmed parts into another block.

2. Add sashing strips to the bottoms of 64 blocks as shown.

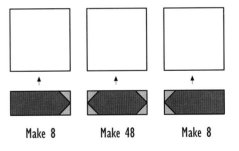

Make 8   Make 48   Make 8

3. Arrange the sashed blocks and sashing strips, alternating rows of 9 blocks each with a vertical sashing row. Make sure the blocks with points on only one end are in the outer rows, and the blocks with no sashing strips attached are at the bottoms of the block rows. Sew the blocks together in vertical rows.

Looking Back...

The "contained" Crazy quilt is the predecessor of the heavily embellished and decorative silk and satin Crazy quilts of the 1890s and 1900s. These early Crazy quilts were nearly as similar to the Sampler quilt as to the true Crazy quilt. Sampler blocks or unused pattern blocks were expanded or trimmed to fit the block format, providing a more restrained look than a true Crazy quilt, which has no recognizable block patterns. The blocks of a contained Crazy quilt are confined within a grid, making the quilt look more orderly than the side-by-side block settings of the later Crazy quilts. Often, the sashing, rather than the blocks of these earlier Crazy quilts, became the focal point.

Instead of the embroidery and fancy fabrics featured in the later, better-known, Victorian Crazy quilts, contained Crazy quilts were made from all-cotton recycled shirtings and women's print dresses, including mourning prints, double pinks, indigos, browns, and homespuns.

By the 1890s, the lavishly embroidered and embellished Victorian Crazy quilts were so popular that women's magazines printed instructions, women collected silk cigarette papers for their quilts, and every well-decorated Victorian home had a Crazy-quilt throw on the fainting couch.

Like every fad, Crazy quilts became extreme. Some were overwhelming and garish. Many of these silk, satin, and velvet quilts survive today because they were strictly decorative and never washed. However, silks used for clothing were treated with a salt solution to make them stiff enough to hold the shape of elaborate leg-o'-mutton sleeves and bustles of the era. Most of the treated silks in Crazy quilts have disintegrated, while the other fabrics remain intact.

4. Sew the rows of blocks and sashing strips together.

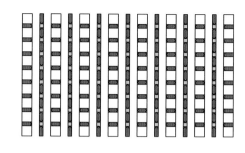

Finishing

Refer to pages 91–95 for information on finishing your quilt.

1. Mark the quilt top with quilting designs as desired.
2. Layer the quilt top with batting and backing.
3. Baste, quilt, and bind.
4. Label your Contained Crazy quilt.

Rose of Sharon with Birds

This quilt, made in the 1850s, is unusual because it combines the fine needlework of more formal appliqué quilts with folk art–style elements (the plants and birds).

Reproduction designed by Lisa DeBee Schiller.

Finished Size: 85" x 104" • Block Size: 19" x 19"

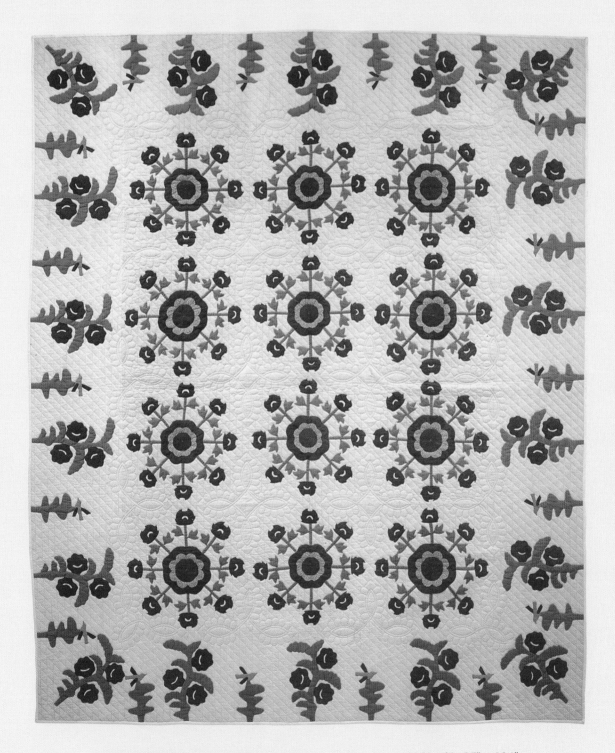

Rose of Sharon with Birds by unknown quilter, circa 1850–60, 85" x 104".

Materials: 44"-wide fabric

8 yds. off-white for background
4½ yds. green solid for stems and leaves
3 yds. red solid for flowers and bird wings
⅜ yd. pink print for flowers
¼ yd. gold solid for birds
9¾ yds. for backing
¾ yd. for binding
90" x 110" piece of batting
Freezer paper

Cutting

Use the diagrams on the pullout pattern. Refer to "Freezer-Paper Appliqué" on pages 85–86 to prepare templates.

From off-white fabric, cut:
12 squares, each 22" x 22"

10 strips, each 14½" x 42". Sew end to end and crosscut into:
2 strips, each 14½" x 57½"
2 strips, each 14½" x 104½"

From green solid fabric, cut:
96 Template #1
96 Template #1 reversed
96 Template #2
18 Template #8
18 Template #9

From red solid fabric, cut:
96 Template #3
18 Template #7
36 Template #7 reversed
12 Template #4
12 Template #6
36 Template #11

From pink print, cut:
12 Template #5

From gold solid fabric, cut:
18 Template #10

Assembling the Blocks

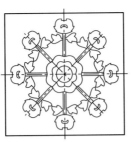

1. Mark reverse appliqué lines on the right side of pieces #3 and #7.
2. Draw a full-size pattern of the block from the partial block on the pullout pattern. Center a background block over the appliqué motif and lightly trace appliqué placement lines onto the background block.
3. Pin or baste the prepared appliqué pieces (with freezer paper inside) to the background blocks in numerical order.
4. Appliqué all pieces to the block backgrounds.
5. Cut out the area of reverse appliqué on each flower, leaving a scant ¼"-wide seam allowance. Turn under and stitch the flower to the background around the opening.
6. Make slits in the background behind the appliqué pieces and remove the freezer paper.

7. Trim the blocks to 19½" x 19½".

Assembling the Quilt Top

1. Sew the blocks together side by side into 4 rows of 3.
2. Sew the rows together.

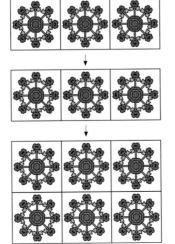

Adding the Borders

1. Sew the 14½" x 57½" border strips to the top and bottom of the quilt top.
2. Sew the 14½" x 104½" border strips to the sides of the quilt top.
3. Referring to the border design on the photo and the quilt plan, use a sharp pencil to lightly trace the placement lines for the border appliqué motifs onto the border strips.
4. Mark the placement for the large plants diagonally in each corner.

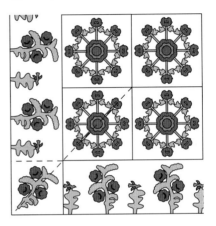

5. Baste or pin and appliqué the plants, flowers, and then birds to the border strips. Notice that each border flower has a shape within it that you reverse-appliqué to the background as you did for the block flowers.

Finishing

Refer to pages 91–95 for information on finishing your quilt.

1. Mark the quilt top for quilting as desired.
2. Layer quilt top with batting and backing.
3. Baste, quilt, and bind.
4. Label your Rose of Sharon quilt.

Basket of Yo-yo Flowers

The original Basket of Yo-yo Flowers, circa 1925–35, is an appliquéd quilt with a playful folk-art feeling. The almost free-form appliqué pieces and the use of yo-yos for the flower centers make this quilt unusual. Reproduction designed by Rachael Lambrecht.

Finished Size: 89½" x 89½" • Block Size: 16" x 16" (23" x 23" on point)

Basket of Yo-yo Flowers, 89½" x 89½".

Materials: 44"-wide fabric

7 yds. muslin for blocks, setting triangles, corner triangles, and borders

2⅔ yds. green solid for leaves, stems, and baskets

1½ yds. red solid for large yo-yos, small yo-yos, and flower buds

½ yd. pink print for large background flower

¼ yd. yellow solid for buds and yo-yo centers

3 yds. green print for sashing and ice cream border

8¼ yds. for backing

1 yd. Nile green for binding

98" x 98" piece of batting

Paper-backed fusible web or freezer paper

Embroidery floss in green, red, pink, and yellow

Cutting

Use the templates on the pullout pattern. Using the appliqué method of your choice, prepare templates and cut out the appliqué pieces. (See pages 85–88.)

From muslin, cut:

13 squares, each 18" x 18"

2 squares, each 26¾" x 26¾". Crosscut twice diagonally for side setting triangles.

2 squares, each 15⅛" x 15⅛". Crosscut once diagonally for corner triangles.

72 Template #16 for ice cream cone border

4 Template #18 for border corners

NOTE: The pattern for this quilt includes an ice cream cone border on all sides.

From green solid fabric, cut:
13 Template #2
104 Template #3
39 Template #4
52 Template #5
13 Template #10
13 Template #10 reversed
13 Template #11

From red solid fabric, cut:
26 Template #7
13 Template #9
13 Template #9 reversed
104 Template #13
13 Template #15

From pink print, cut:
13 Template #1

From yellow solid fabric, cut:
26 Template #6
13 Template #8
13 Template #8 reversed
104 Template #12
13 Template #14

From green print, cut:
18 strips, each 2½" x 42". Crosscut 8 strips into 18 pieces, each 2½" x 16½", for sashing.
76 Template #17 for ice cream cone border

Assembling the Blocks

1. Referring to the full-size design on the pullout pattern, fuse all appliqué pieces, except the yo-yos, to the background blocks in numerical order. Exact placement is not crucial as this is a folk-art project.
2. Buttonhole-stitch around fused pieces with embroidery floss.

Making the Yo-yos

1. Fuse or baste the inside large yellow yo-yo circles to the centers of the wrong side of the large red yo-yo circles.
2. Thread a needle with a double strand of regular thread. Knot the end.

With the wrong side of a yo-yo circle facing up, turn under a scant ¼" as you sew a row of running stitches completely around the circle, close to the folded edge. It is not necessary to make the stitches tiny.

3. Gather the stitches tightly to close the circle and create the yo-yo. Knot the thread and clip. Flatten the yo-yo so the yellow center shows. Repeat for the small yo-yos.

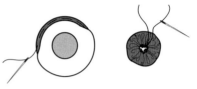

4. Sew the yo-yos to the appliquéd block.

Assembling the Quilt Top

1. Trim the blocks to 16½".
2. Sew the 2½" x 42" sashing strips together, end to end, and crosscut into:
   2 strips, each 2½" x 92½"
   2 strips, each 2½" x 56½"
   2 strips, each 2½" x 20½"
3. Arrange the blocks with setting triangles, corner triangles, and sashing strips. Sew the blocks and setting triangles together into rows, then sew the rows together with the long sashing strips between them. Add the corner triangles last.

Adding the Borders

1. Sew pieces #16 and #17 together into pairs.

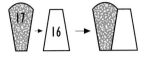

2. Sew together 18 pairs for each of the 4 border strips. Add an extra green piece #17 to the right end of each border so that each strip begins and ends with a green piece #17.

3. Attach ice cream cone border strips to the top and bottom and then to the sides of the quilt. The original quilt has no corners, but you may wish to add the corner pieces (Template #18) to the side borders before attaching them to the quilt.

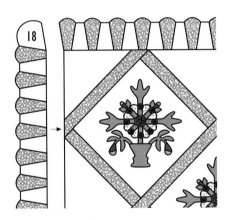

Finishing

Refer to pages 91–95 for information on finishing your quilt.

1. Mark the quilt top with quilting designs as desired.

2. Layer the quilt top with backing and batting.

3. Baste, quilt, and bind with bias binding around the scalloped edges.

4. Label your Basket of Yo-yo Flowers quilt.

Looking Back…

Along with Cathedral Windows, yo-yos were novelties that enjoyed popularity in the 1930s. Newspapers featured craft techniques in articles geared toward women. Novel quiltmaking techniques such as yo-yos were popularized in these publications. Yo-yos appear in many quilts from this era and were often sewed together side by side to create an open-worked bed coverlet with no batting or backing. Yo-yo quilts were faddish and purely decorative. They have periodically appeared in vests, jackets, or as part of an appliqué pattern.

The American International Quilt Association

My family and I founded the American International
Quilt Association (AIQA), and Great Expectations
funded it for the first year. Great Expectations has housed
AIQA for most of its fifteen years and provides fabrics for
many of the handsome AIQA raffle quilts that help earn money
for the organization. Now AIQA is housed at the Quilts,
Inc., corporate offices.

Founders' Star

Founders' Star combines deep red, navy blue, and cream fabrics in a unique five-pointed Feathered Star Medallion design. Designed by Jewel Pearce Patterson.

Finished Size: 99¼" x 99¼"

Founders' Star, *designed by Jewel Pearce Patterson, 1986, Houston, Texas, 99¼" x 99¼". Founders' Star was created as a fund-raiser for the Texas Sesquicentennial Quilt Search.*

Materials: 44"-wide fabric

4 yds. red print
4¾ yds. blue print
8 yds. cream solid
9 yds. for backing
⅞ yd. blue for binding
110" x 110" piece of batting

Cutting

Cut lengthwise strips parallel to the selvages first. Then cut crosswise strips across the fabric width from selvage to selvage. Cut the other pieces from the remaining fabric. Use the templates on the pullout pattern.

From red print, cut:

4 lengthwise strips, each 1½" x 44", for border 2

4 lengthwise strips, each 1½" x 52", for border 4

4 lengthwise strips, each 1½" x 64", for border 6

4 crosswise strips, each 4⅝" x 42". Crosscut into 28 squares, each 4⅝" x 4⅝". Cut once diagonally for border 9 block corners.

4 squares, each 6¼" x 6¼". Cut once diagonally for border 9 corner triangles.

1 square, 35½" x 35½", for center block background

1 Template #1 for pentagon center

88 Template #7 for Texas Tears border 5

8 Template #11 for Texas Tears border 9 corner blocks

From blue print, cut:

4 lengthwise strips, each 2" x 77", for border 8

4 lengthwise strips, each 2" x 101", for border 10

3 crosswise strips, each 3⅜" x 42". Crosscut into 30 squares, each 3⅜" x 3⅜". Cut once diagonally for half-square triangles of sawtooth border 1.

13 crosswise strips, each 1¾" x 42", for border 9 Ninepatch blocks

5 crosswise strips, each 2⅛" x 42". Crosscut into 84 squares and cut once diagonally for border 9 half-square triangles.

5 Template #2 for center star points
90 Template #3 for star feathers
5 Template #5 for star tips
88 Template #7 for Texas Tears border 5
8 Template #11 for Texas Tears border 9
   corner blocks

From cream solid fabric, cut:

4 lengthwise strips, each 3½" x 50", for
   border 3

4 lengthwise strips, each 5¼" x 74", for
   border 7

3 crosswise strips, each 3⅜" x 42". Crosscut into 30 squares, each 3⅜" x 3⅜". Cut
   once diagonally for border 1 half-square
   triangles.

11 crosswise strips, each 1¾" x 42", for border 9 Ninepatch units

9 crosswise strips, each 2⅛" x 42". Crosscut into 168 squares, each 2⅛" x 2⅛",
   and cut once diagonally for border 9 half-
   square triangles.

12 squares, each 11⅞" x 11⅞". Crosscut twice
   diagonally for border 9 side triangles.

12 squares, each 6¼" x 6¼". Cut once diagonally for border 9 corner triangles.

80 Template #3

10 Template #4

5 Template #6 for background of center star

For Texas Tears border 5:

80 Template #8
4 Template #9
4 Template #9 reversed
4 Template #10
4 Template #10 reversed
16 Template #12

Assembling the Center Medallion

1. Using the blue and cream piece #3 triangles, make 5 of each type of feather strip
as shown for the sides of the star points.

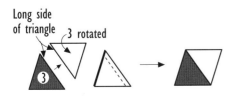

2. Sew the feather strips to the star points.
Sew a piece #4 to the sides of the piece #5
star tips. Add a star-tip unit to each star
point.

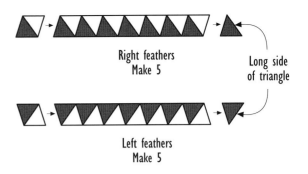

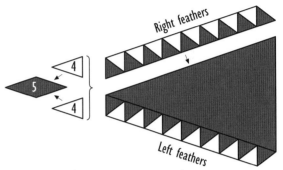

3. Sew the star points to the center pentagon, beginning and ending ¼" from the
side edge.

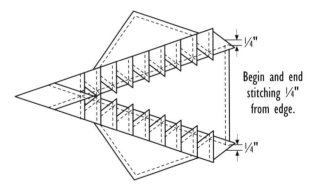

4. Finish the star by sewing the seams between each star point.

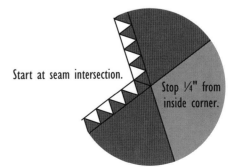

Alice's Hot Fudge Sundae Cake

1 cup flour
¾ cup sugar
2 Tablespoons cocoa
2 teaspoons baking powder
¼ teaspoon salt
½ cup milk
2 Tablespoons salad oil
1 teaspoon vanilla
1 cup chopped nuts (optional)

Preheat oven to 350° F. Stir together flour, sugar, cocoa, baking powder, and salt in a 9" x 9" x 2" pan. Add milk, oil, and vanilla to pan. Mix ingredients with a fork until smooth. Stir in chopped nuts if desired. Spread mixture evenly in pan. Set aside while making topping.

Topping

1 cup packed brown sugar
¼ cup cocoa
1¾ cups hot tap water
Ice cream

Sprinkle brown sugar and cocoa evenly over cake mixture in pan. Pour hot tap water over top.

Bake for 40 minutes. Let stand for 15 minutes. Cut into squares. Invert a square on a plate. Top with a scoop of ice cream and spoon sauce from pan over ice cream.

5. Sew a cream piece #6 between each pair of star points, matching the seam intersections.

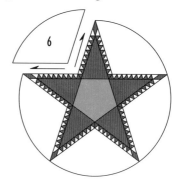

6. Center the cream star circle on the 35½" x 35½" red background square; appliqué in place.

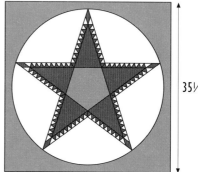

35½"

Assembling the Borders

Border 1

1. To construct the 2½"-wide sawtooth border, sew the cream and blue 3⅜" triangles together into half-square triangle units.

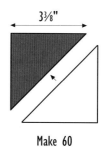

3⅜"

Make 60

2. Sew the units together into strips of 14 units each, with blue triangles of 7 units facing one way and 7 facing the other way.

3. Sew strips to the top and bottom of the center square.

4. Add a half-square triangle unit to the 2 remaining sawtooth strips, rotating the

squares as shown. Sew the strips to the sides of the center square.

Borders 2, 3, and 4

1. Fold the following strips in half and mark the centers of the seam allowances: the 1½" x 44" red strips, the 3½" x 50" cream strips, and the 1½" x 52" red strips. Sew 1 of each strip together, matching the center marks, and treat the resulting unit as one border strip.

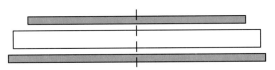

Match centers of strips.

2. Referring to pages 90–91, sew the triple border strips to the quilt top and miter the corners.

Border 5

1. To construct the Texas Tears border, be sure to mark the seam intersections on the template pieces as you cut them out. Sew a blue piece #7 to a red piece #7, stitching from edge to the seam intersection as shown.

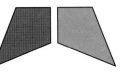

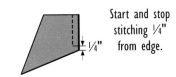

Start and stop stitching ¼" from edge.

Quilts were often used as fundraisers for the community. Groups of women made quilts for flood relief, to raise money for the local church or school, or as a parting gift for a retiring minister. Many of these quilts had embroidered or inked signatures. Individuals paid for the privilege of signing the blocks, then the quilt was raffled to the highest bidder when completed.

Groups of quilters have used quilts to raise money to help the troops in every U.S. war, to improve the environment, to buy books for libraries and equipment for schools. Today, quilt guilds make quilts for babies with AIDS, to raise money for local charities, and to give to the homeless.

In this time-honored tradition, the four founders of the nonprofit American International Quilt Association, Texans all, made the Founders' Star quilt to raise money to further the goals of the organization. The Founders' Star was the AIQA raffle quilt for 1986, the year of the Texas Sesquicentennial.

2. Sew pairs of piece #7 together to make 40 stars.

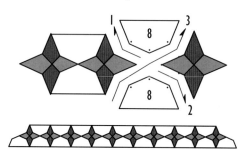

Make 40

3. Sew a star to a piece #8, matching seam intersections. Repeat with another star and piece #8. Then sew the 2 units together in one long seam, carefully matching the seam intersections.

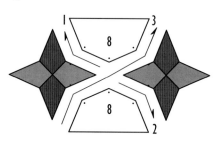

4. Continue adding pieces until the strip has 10 stars and 20 of piece #8.

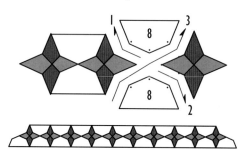

5. To complete the left end of each border, join a red piece #7, a blue piece #7, a cream piece #9, and a cream piece #10 as shown. Add the unit to the left end of the border.

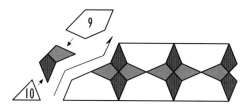

6. To complete the right end of the border strip, join a red piece #7, a blue piece #7, a cream piece #9 reversed, and a cream piece #10 reversed as shown. Add the unit

to the right end of the border.

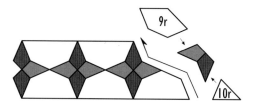

7. Sew the border strips to the quilt top, beginning and ending your stitching ¼" from the corners. Sew the border strips together, stitching from the inside corner out to the edge.

Borders 6, 7, and 8

1. Fold the following strips in half and mark the centers of the seam allowances: the 1½" x 64" red strips, the 5¼" x 74" cream strips, and the 2" x 77" blue strips. Sew 1 of each strip together, matching the center marks, and treat the resulting unit as one border strip.

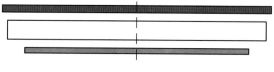

Match centers of strips.

2. Referring to pages 90–91, sew the triple border strips to the quilt top and miter the corners.

Border 9

1. To construct the blocks for the 10⅝"-wide border 9, sew the 1¾" x 42" blue and cream strips together to make 2 strip sets. Press the seams toward the blue strips.

2. Cut the strip sets into 1¾"-wide segments and piece Ninepatch blocks as shown.

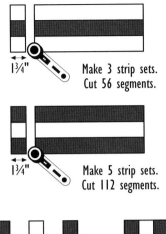

Make 3 strip sets.
Cut 56 segments.

Make 5 strip sets.
Cut 112 segments.

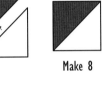

Make 56

3. Sew the 2⅛" cream and blue half-square triangles together to make half-square triangle units.

Make 8

4. Assemble 3 half-square triangle units, 3 cream triangles, and a red 4⅝" triangle as shown to make a triangle unit.

Make 56

5. Sew the Ninepatch units and triangle units together.

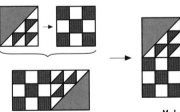

Make 28

6. Sew the 11⅞" cream triangles to the sides of the blocks as shown.

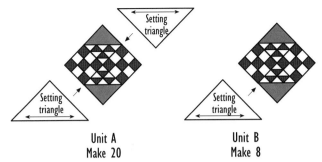

Unit A
Make 20

Unit B
Make 8

7. Assemble 5 Unit A and 2 Unit B into a strip. Add cream 6¼" triangles to complete the border strip (shown below).

8. Sew pieced border strips to the top and bottom of the quilt top.

9. To make Texas Tears corner blocks, join blue and red #11 pieces and cream piece #12 as in border 5, steps 1–4 on pages 59–60. Add red and cream 6¼" triangles.

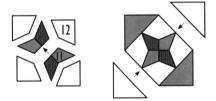

10. Add Texas Tears corner blocks to the ends of the 2 remaining pieced border strips and sew them to the sides of the quilt top.

Border 10

Referring to pages 90–91, add the 2"-wide blue border strips to the quilt top and miter the corners.

Finishing

Refer to pages 91–95 for information on finishing your quilt.

1. Mark the quilt top with quilting designs as desired.

2. Layer the quilt top with batting and backing.

3. Baste, quilt, and bind.

4. Label your Founders' Star quilt.

Corner

Corner

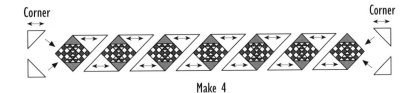

Make 4

The Texas Quilt Search

In 1986 Texas celebrated its 150th birthday as a republic—its Sesquicentennial. My cousin Nancy, our friend Suzanne Yabsley, and I wanted to ensure that women's contributions to the state were recognized. We formed the Texas Sesquicentennial Quilt Association (TSQA) in 1980, and Nancy and I covered thousands of miles to find, document, exhibit, and catalog Texas quilts made before 1836. Great Expectations was the collection point for all of the quilts and provided office and work space for TSQA. By the end of our initial travel and research, we had documented 3,500 quilts. A book, "Lone Stars: A Legacy of Texas Quilts, 1836—1936," featured highlights of the search. Our ongoing documentation efforts cataloged another 1,500 quilts, and, in 1990, resulted in a second volume, "Lone Stars Two: A Legacy of Texas Quilts, 1936—1986."

Blue Carpenter's Square

The success of this design depends on the illusion
of the strips weaving over and under each other across
the quilt. Be sure to match the strips carefully.

Finished Size: 69" x 69" • Block Size: 23" x 23"

Left to right (opposite): Karey Bresenhan, Nancy O'Bryant, then-Governor Mark White, Suzanne Yabsley, and Kathleen McCrady, holding the quilted version of the logo for the Sesquicentennial. Photo by Bill Malone. **Blue Carpenter's Square** *by unknown quilter, circa 1880–90, 69" x 69".*

Materials: 44"-wide fabric

3¼ yds. blue print
3 yds. white-on-white print
4½ yds. for backing
⅝ yd. for binding
75" x 75" piece of batting

Cutting

From blue print, cut:
    27 strips, each 1¾" x 42". Crosscut strips
        into 54 pieces, each 1¾" x 16¾"
    36 strips, each 1¾" x 42", for strip units

From white-on-white print, cut:
    24 strips, each 1¾" x 42", for strip units
    12 strips, each 4¼" x 42". Crosscut 9 strips
        into 36 rectangles, each 4¼" x 9".

TIP: When you sew together a two-color, high-contrast quilt, use two colors of thread—one in the bobbin and one on top.

Assembling the Blocks

1. Sew together 12 sets of 1¾-wide" blue and white strips as shown.

6¾"

Make 12 strip units.

2. Crosscut 6 of the strip units into 36 segments, each 6¾" x 6¾".

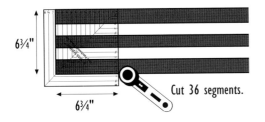

6¾"

6¾"

Cut 36 segments.

3. Cut 18 of the segments diagonally from upper left corner to lower right corner, and cut 18 segments from upper right corner to lower left corner to yield a total of 36 pieced triangles of each.

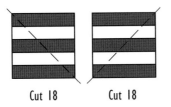

Cut 18   Cut 18

4. To make the block corners, sew a pieced triangle to each side of a 4¼" x 9" white print rectangle as shown.

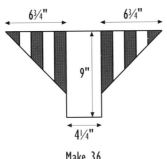

6¾"   6¾"

9"

4¼"

Make 36

5. Sew 2 of the remaining strip units to a 4¼"-wide strip of white print as shown.

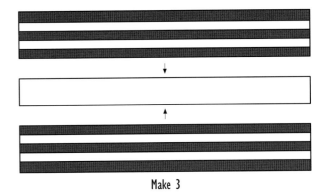

Make 3

6. From the strip units assembled in step 5, cut:
36 segments, each 1¾" x 16¾"
9 segments, each 4¼" x 16¾"

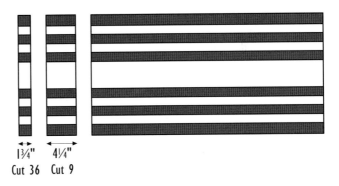

1¾"   4¼"
Cut 36   Cut 9

7. Assemble the segments with the 1¾" x 16¾" blue strips to make the block centers.

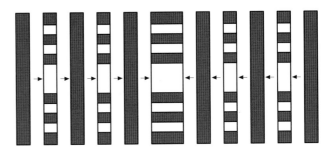

Texas Trifle

This is a great low-calorie dessert—pretty, tasty, and showy! Do not prepare your trifle more than a few hours before serving, or the fruit and the yogurt mixture will change texture.

1 angel food cake
2 pints fresh strawberries
1 pint fresh blueberries
1 large package frozen blackberries (without sugar)
1 large package frozen peaches (without sugar)
12 or more packets of Equal® artificial sweetener
1 medium container non-fat plain yogurt
Vanilla to taste

Tear cake into medium pieces and set aside. Wipe off strawberries with a damp paper towel. (NEVER wash strawberries—they absorb water like little red sponges!) Cut off hulls and let the berries dry on paper towels, stem end down. Rinse the blueberries and drain in a colander till dry. Slightly defrost frozen fruits but leave them icy.

Mash ½ pint strawberries (a pastry blender works well). Add Equal to strawberries and blend gently. Add strawberry/Equal mixture to yogurt. Add a splash or two of vanilla. Taste. Add more Equal if desired. Yogurt mixture will be a beautiful rosy-pink.

Layer the cake, fruit, and yogurt sauce in a trifle dish or pretty glass bowl. Start with a layer of cake pieces, then alternate layers of fruit, yogurt, and cake. End with a layer of yogurt and top with whole berries. Cover tightly and chill thoroughly, about 3 hours.

8. Add corner units to each side of the center square and trim the corners using a Bias Square® ruler.

Assembling the Quilt Top

1. Arrange the blocks side by side in 3 rows of 3; sew them together into rows, matching seams carefully.
2. Sew the rows together, matching the seams in the adjoining blocks.

Finishing

Refer to pages 91–95 for information on finishing your quilt.

1. Mark the quilt top with quilting designs as desired.
2. Layer the quilt top with batting and backing.
3. Baste, quilt, and bind.
4. Label your Blue Carpenter's Square quilt.

Red Carpenter's Square

Finished Size: 73" x 73"

Red Carpenter's Square *by the same unknown quilter who made the Blue Carpenter's Square on page 63, circa 1880–90, 73" x 73".*

Materials: 44"-wide fabric

3¾ yds. white
2¾ yds. red
4½ yds. white for backing
⅝ yd. red for binding
80" x 80" piece of batting

Cutting

From white fabric, cut:
22 strips, each 1½" x 42"
1 strip, 2½" x 42"
1 strip, 3½" x 42"
1 strip, 4½" x 42"
5 strips, each 5½" x 43"
7 strips, each 6½" x 42"
5 squares, each 5½" x 5½", for piece A
2 strips, each 5½" x 17½", for piece B
6 pieces, each 5½" x 6½", for piece C
2 pieces, each 5½" x 10½", for Block 5
From red fabric, cut:
61 strips, each 1½" x 42"

Assembling the Blocks

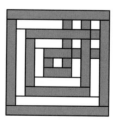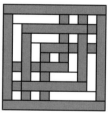

Block 1   Block 2

Blocks 1 and 2

1. Sew 1½"-wide white and red strips together as shown. Crosscut the strip unit into 1½"-wide segments.

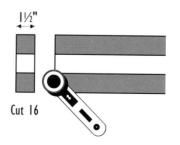

1½"

Cut 16

2. To make the block centers, cut 3 red strips into 32 pieces, each 1½" x 3½"; sew to opposite sides of the strip-pieced segments.

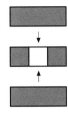

Make 16

3. Cut a 1½"-wide white strip into 12 pieces, each 1½" x 3½", and sew to the left side of the block centers for Block 1 as shown.

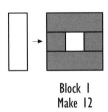

Block 1
Make 12

4. Sew a red strip and a 2½"-wide white strip together. Crosscut into 1½"-wide segments. Sew a segment to the right side of Block 1 and to both sides of Block 2.

1½"

Cut 32

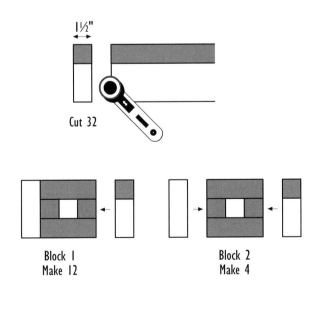

Block 1
Make 12

Block 2
Make 4

5. Sew together a 3½"-wide white strip, a red strip, and a 1½"-wide white strip. Crosscut into 1½"-wide segments. Sew segments to the top of Block 1 and to the top and bottom of Block 2.

1½"

Cut 20

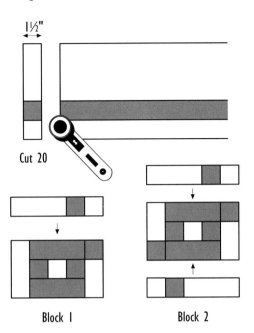

Block 1

Block 2

6. From the 1½"-wide white strips, cut 12 pieces, 1½" x 5½". Sew a piece to the bottom of Block 1.

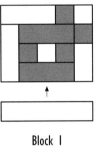

Block 1

7. From the red strips, cut 32 pieces, each 1½" x 5½". Sew pieces to both sides of Block 1 and Block 2.

8. From the red strips, cut 32 pieces, each 1½" x 7½". Sew pieces to the top and bottom of Block 1 and Block 2.

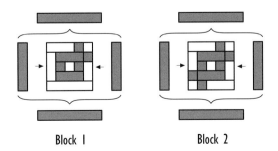

Block 1

Block 2

Cherry Cream Cheese Christmas Cake

1 8-oz. package cream cheese
1 cup margarine or butter
1½ cups sugar
1½ teaspoons vanilla
4 eggs
2¼ cups sifted cake flour
1½ teaspoons baking powder
¾ cup (8-oz. jar) well-drained, chopped maraschino cherries
1 cup chopped pecans
¾ cup finely chopped pecans

Preheat oven to 325° F. Soften cream cheese and butter. Add sugar and vanilla and blend well. Add eggs, one at a time, and mix well after each addition. Sift 2 cups cake flour with baking powder and gradually add to cream cheese mixture.

Combine the remaining flour with cherries and 1 cup chopped pecans. Fold into batter.

Grease a 10-inch Bundt pan or tube pan. Sprinkle pan with ¾ cup finely chopped pecans. Pour batter into pan. Bake for 70–75 minutes. (Do not overbake!) Cool 5 minutes; remove from pan. Glaze and decorate.

Confectioner's Sugar Glaze

1½ cups sifted confectioner's sugar
2 Tablespoons milk
Red maraschino cherries
Pecan halves

Combine confectioner's sugar and milk. Drizzle over top and sides of cake. Decorate with cherries and pecan halves.

9. From the 1½"-wide white strips, cut 12 pieces, each 1½" x 7½". Add a piece to the left side of each Block 1.

Block 1

10. Sew together a red strip, a 1½"-wide white strip, a red strip, and a 4½"-wide white strip as shown. Crosscut into 1½"-wide segments. Sew a segment to the right side of Block 1 and to the right and left sides of Block 2.

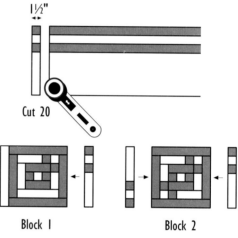

1½"
Cut 20

Block 1   Block 2

11. Sew together a 1½"-wide white strip, a red strip, a 1½"-wide white strip, a red strip, and a 5½"-wide white strip as shown. Crosscut into 1½"-wide segments. Add a segment to the top of Block 1 and to the top and bottom of Block 2.

12. Cut four 1½"-wide white strips into 12 pieces, each 1½" x 9½". Sew a piece to the bottom of Block 1.

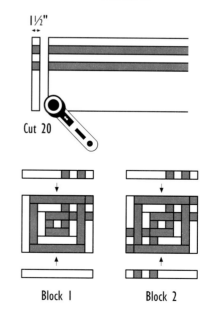

1½"
Cut 20

Block 1   Block 2

13. Cut 8 red strips into 32 pieces, each 1½" x 9½". Sew a piece to both sides of Block 1 and Block 2.

14. Cut 11 red strips into 32 pieces, each 1½" x 11½". Add a strip to the top and bottom of Block 1 and Block 2.

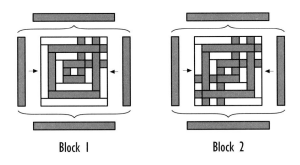

Block 1   Block 2

Blocks 3, 4, 5, and 6

1. Sew a red strip and a 5½"-wide white strip together. Make 2 sets and crosscut them into 8 segments, each 5½" wide.

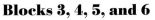

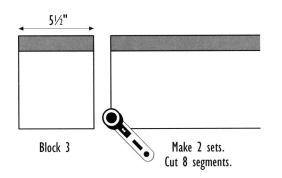

Block 3   Make 2 sets.
                 Cut 8 segments.

2. Sew together a red strip, a 1½"-wide white strip, a red strip, a 1½"-wide white strip, and a red strip. Make 3 sets and crosscut into 20 segments, each 5½" wide.

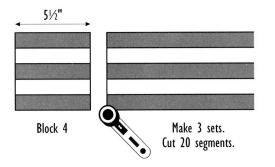

Block 4   Make 3 sets.
                 Cut 20 segments.

Looking Back...

The kind of woman who made quilts such as these two Carpenter's Squares was meant to be an engineer or an architect. Unfortunately, these careers were not as open to women of the 1880s as they are today. Then all of a woman's talents were funneled into domestic life. It is only natural that a woman with mathematical abilities and interests would not long be satisfied with sewing simple quilt patterns. Complicated patterns, such as New York Beauty, Mariner's Compass, Five-Pointed Star, and Feathered Star, must have been drafted by women who needed a challenge. These women were able to show off their engineering abilities by making geometrically intricate quilts. Quiltmakers may not have known the math involved in their quilt patterns, nor did they have calculators to figure the measurements. Some may have used drafting tools, but most relied on folded paper patterns and an artist's eye for balance.

3. From a red strip, cut 2 segments, each 1½" x 5½". Sew a red segment to one end of the 5½" x 10½" white pieces as shown.

5½" x 10½"

1½" x 5½"

Block 5

4. From a red strip, cut 2 segments, each 1½" x 5½". Cut a 5½"-wide white strip into 2 segments, each 5½" x 21½". Sew a red segment to one end of the white segments as shown.

5½" x 21½"

1½" x 5½"

Block 6

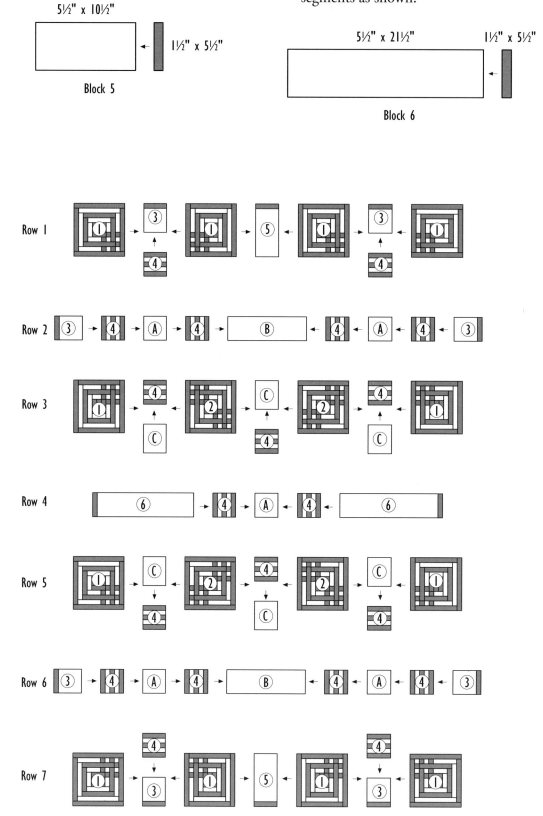

Row 1

Row 2

Row 3

Row 4

Row 5

Row 6

Row 7

Assembling the Quilt Top

1. Arrange the blocks and pieces of white fabric as shown below. Sew them together into rows.
2. Sew the rows together, matching the seams carefully.

Adding the Borders

1. Sew the 7 white 6½"-wide border strips together end to end. Crosscut into:
   2 strips, each 6½" x 59½"
   2 strips, each 6½" x 71½"
2. Sew the 59½"-long strips to the top and bottom of the quilt top. Sew the 71½"-long strips to the sides.
3. Sew the 7 remaining red strips together end to end. Crosscut into:
   2 strips, each 1½" x 71½"
   2 strips, each 1½" x 73½"
4. Sew the 71½"-long strips to the top and bottom of the quilt top. Sew the 73½"-long strips to the sides.

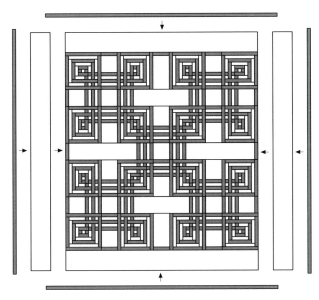

Finishing

Refer to pages 91–95 for information on finishing your quilt.

1. Mark the quilt top with quilting designs as desired.
2. Layer the quilt top with batting and backing.
3. Baste, quilt, and bind.
4. Label your Red Carpenter's Square quilt.

Looking Back...

Traditional patterns often have special meanings based more on the name of the block than its appearance. It is hard to discern why a quiltmaker would name a star block with four-patch corners "54-40 or Fight." The appearance of that block seems to have little to do with the name's political statement, which was an argument for the United States to extend its border to the 54th parallel. Women did not participate in important political debates before they were allowed to vote, but they had opinions, which they expressed in quilt patterns such as Clay's Choice, Whig Rose, Kansas Troubles, and Underground Railroad. Like many other blocks with political names, "54-40 or Fight" is widely used and known to quilters today, but the political meaning behind the name is not.

Religion was another common theme, and many quilt patterns have religious names, such as Jacob's Ladder, Crown of Thorns, and Tree of Life.

Life was hard for the women who migrated west with their husbands, and that harshness is reflected in the names they gave to their quilt blocks, such as Rocky Road to Kansas, Texas Tears, Rocky Mountain Road, and Kansas Dugout.

All aspects of women's lives are included in the quilts they made and named: their political and religious views, the hardships they endured, the artifacts of their daily lives, and the stars over their heads.

International Friends

At Great Expectations, we have always appreciated our visitors from foreign countries and have frequently gone to extraordinary lengths to bring our international friends to the shop. When people look at quilts, they don't have to have words in common, because quilts have become their international language. International communication is what European Quilt Market and Quilt Expo in Europe are all about.

The interest in international quilts began at the October 1985 International Quilt Festival with a single exhibit. "Hands All Around: Quilts From Many Nations," that featured fifty quilts by forty-two quiltmakers from seventeen countries. It was sponsored by Quilter's Newsletter Magazine and curated by magazine publisher Bonnie Leman and me. The exhibit inspired a book by the same name, written by Bonnie and me, with Robert Bishop, the late director of the Museum of American Folk Art. Research for the book initiated contact with many quilters and quilt lovers who helped as European Quilt Market and Quilt Expo were established.

The first European Quilt Market for retailers and the first Quilt Expo for consumers was held in 1988 in Salzburg, Austria. Since then, they have been held in Scheveningen and The Hague, The Netherlands; Odense, Denmark; Antwerp and Brussels, Belgium; and Karlsruhe, Germany. The 1996 European Quilt market and Quilt Expo will take place in Lyon, France.

Tulip Time

Pattern for center medallion with
borders designed by Jewel Pearce Patterson.

Finished Quilt Size: 75½" x 75½" • Finished Center Medallion Size: 27" x 27"

*Tulip Time, Jewel's Center Medallion by Jewel Pearce Patterson, 1992
(finished quilt size 75½" x 75½"). Jewel (Karey's mother) created a medallion quilt as a fund-raiser
for Quilt Expo in Holland. (Owned by Kari Smedsass, Norway)*

Materials: 44"-wide fabric

½ yd. off-white for background square, pinwheels, border, and backing
⅛-yd. pieces of assorted tulip colors, such as yellow, true red, peach, pink, purple—2 shades of each color for each flower
⅓ yd. medium green for stems
1¼ yds. dark green solid for leaves, stems, and sashing
⅛ yd. red solid for pinwheels
4⅞ yds. for backing
¼ yd. for binding
84" x 84" piece of batting

Cutting

Use the templates on the pullout pattern. Using the appliqué method of your choice, prepare templates and cut out the appliqué pieces. (See pages 85–88.)

From off-white fabric, cut:
1 square, 16½" x 16½", for background
4 pieces, each 4" x 18½", for borders
8 squares, each 2⅝" x 2⅝". Crosscut once diagonally for half-square triangles.

From assorted colors for tulips, cut:
1 each of Templates #9–#22 in your choice of colors with 2 shades for each flower

From medium green fabric, cut:
14 bias strips, each 1½" x 12", for stems
1 each of Templates #1–#8

From dark green solid fabric, cut:
5 strips, each 1½" x 42". Sew strips end to end and crosscut into:
2 strips, each 1½" x 16½"
2 strips, each 1½" x 18½"
2 strips, each 1½" x 25½"
2 strips, each 1½" x 27½"

From red solid fabric, cut:
8 squares, each 2⅝" x 2⅝". Crosscut once diagonally for half-square triangles.

Assembling the Appliqué Block

1. Referring to the instructions for "Making Bias Stems" on page 88, use the ⅜"-wide bias bar to make 14 bias stems, each 12" long, from the medium green bias strips.

2. Using the diagram on page 76 as a guide, lightly mark placement lines for the tulips, stems, and leaves on the background square.

3. Place the appliqué pieces on the background squares in layers. Baste or pin. Appliqué the leaves first, then stems, and flowers last.

Appliqué leaves   then stems   then flowers

Adding the Sashing and Borders

1. Sew the 1½" x 16½" dark green sashing strips to the top and bottom of the completed appliqué block. Add the 1½" x 18½" dark green sashing strips to the sides.

2. To construct pinwheel corner blocks for the border, sew a red half-square triangle to an off-white half-square triangle.

3. Sew 4 squares together as shown to make a pinwheel.

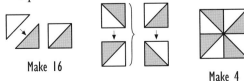

Make 16   Make 4

4. Add the 4" x 18½" white border strips to the top and bottom of the quilt top.

5. Add pinwheel blocks to each end of the remaining white border strips. Sew one to each side of the quilt top.

6. Add a 1½" x 25½" dark green sashing strip to the top and bottom of the quilt top. Add the 1½" x 27½" dark green sashing strips to the sides.

Finishing

Refer to pages 91–95 for information on finishing your quilt.

1. Mark the quilt top with quilting designs as desired.
2. Layer the quilt top with backing and batting.
3. Baste, quilt, and bind.
4. Label your Tulip Time quilt.

The Smithsonian

When the Smithsonian Institution and American Pacific Enterprises began to produce, in China, copies of American quilts from the Smithsonian collections, I saw red. Nancy and I spearheaded a year-long national campaign against it, collecting signatures of 25,000 American quilters from all 50 states on petitions of protest. We hand carried these documents to Washington, D.C., where I testified before Congress and we met with Smithsonian officials. The results were gratifying! The Smithsonian agreed not to renew the licensing agreement that had allowed copies of some of its quilt treasury to be made in China.

I proposed practical, alternative marketing ideas that would generate at least as much revenue for the Smithsonian as the Chinese quilt reproductions but be far more beneficial to the American quilting industry and American quilters. Among the proposals were one or more books of quilt patterns and lines of reproduction fabrics based on Smithsonian quilts.

Another important effect of the Smithsonian controversy was that we recognized the need for an entity to protect the interests of American quilting and quilters. Nancy and I, with two of the founding directors of The Kentucky Quilt Project, founded the Alliance for American Quilts. The Alliance's immediate goals are to establish the American Quilt History Center and the International Quilt Index.

Moss Rose

The directions for the Moss Rose quilt were modified from the original quilt for easier assembly. Reproduction designed by Lisa DeBee Schiller.

Finished Size: 85" x 85" • Block Size: 23" x 23"

Karey Bresenhan and Nancy O'Bryant in Washington, D.C. (opposite). Photo by Timothy A. Murphy.
Moss Rose *by unknown quilter, circa 1850–60, 85" x 85". Moss Rose was hung at International Quilt Festival 1992 beside a Chinese-made copy of a Smithsonian Institution masterpiece to show the difference in workmanship between American-made quilts and imported ones. (Quilts, Inc., Corporate Collection)*

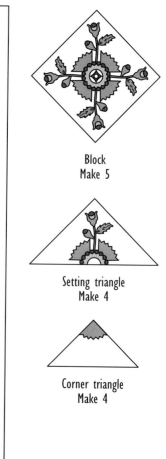

Block
Make 5

Setting triangle
Make 4

Corner triangle
Make 4

Materials: 44"-wide fabric

7¾ yds. off-white for background and borders
4⅝ yds. green solid
1¼ yds. red solid
⅝ yd. pink print
⅛ yd. yellow print
8¼ yds. off-white for backing
¾ yd. off-white for binding
90" x 90" piece of batting
Freezer paper

Cutting

Use the templates on the pullout pattern. Using the appliqué method of your choice, prepare templates and cut out the appliqué pieces. (See pages 85–88.)

From off-white background fabric, cut:
5 squares, each 27" x 27"
1 square, 34" x 34". Crosscut twice diagonally for side setting triangles.
2 squares, each 17¼" x 17¼". Crosscut once diagonally for corner triangles.
2 pieces, each 11" x 65½"
2 pieces, each 11" x 86½"

From green solid fabric, cut:
24 Template #1
24 Template #2
24 Template #7
32 Template #8
24 Template #16
24 Template #17
20 Template #18a
4 Template #18b
24 Template #20
24 Template #26

From red solid fabric, cut:
24 Template #3
24 Template #6
5 Template #9
5 Template #12
4 Template #14
24 Template #21
24 Template #25

From pink print, cut:
24 Template #5
5 Template #10
4 Template #15

From yellow print, cut:
5 Template #11
5 Template #13

Assembling the Blocks

1. Trace the placement lines for the appliqué pieces onto the background squares and triangles using the diagram on the pull-out pattern.

2. Follow the directions on page 88 to make bias stems. Use the ¾"-wide bias strips to make ¼"-wide bias stems. Cut the ¼"-wide bias stems into 24 pieces, each 4½" long. Use the 1¼"-wide bias strips to make ⅜"-wide bias stems. Cut the ⅜"-wide bias stems into 24 pieces, each 8" long.

3. Place the bias stems and appliqué pieces onto the background squares, setting triangles, and corner triangles. Baste or pin in place and appliqué the pieces in numerical order.

4. Measure and trim the blocks to 23½" x 23½".

5. Arrange the blocks, setting triangles, and corner triangles in diagonal rows. Sew the blocks in rows, then sew the rows together, matching seams carefully.

Adding the Borders

Refer to the quilt plan on page 80 for placement of the border appliqués.

1. Sew an 11" x 65½" off-white piece to the top and bottom of the quilt top.

2. Sew an 11" x 86½" off-white piece to each side.

3. Mark the placement lines for the border appliqué pieces using the pattern on the pullout.

4. Place the swag and tassel appliqués on the borders. Place corner tassels (longer version of tassel) in each corner. Baste or pin and appliqué the pieces to the borders.

Note: Capture the whimsy of the original border by turning some of the tassel rosebuds in different directions and adding some of the large bud motifs on the pullout pattern.

Finishing

Refer to pages 91–95 for information on finishing your quilt.

1. Mark the quilt top with quilting designs as desired.

2. Layer the quilt top with batting and backing.

3. Baste, quilt, and bind.

4. Label your Moss Rose quilt.

Basic Quiltmaking

Fabric

Select high-quality, 100% cotton fabrics. They hold their shape well and are easy to handle. Cotton blends are usually more difficult to stitch and press. Although the yardage you buy is 44" wide, in each quilt plan we have calculated the required yardage based on 42 usable inches of fabric to allow for shrinkage.

Some quilts in this book require an assortment of fabrics in small amounts. If you have scraps, feel free to use them and purchase only those fabrics you need for larger pieces, such as sashing and borders. If you are making a quilt with an antique look, use fabrics with a nostalgic feeling. Several lines of reproduction fabrics currently on the market include plaids, conversation prints, bubble gum pinks of the 1880s, and pastel hues and distinctive "feed-sack" fabrics of the 1930s. Solid colors typical of various past eras are also available now.

Keep your quilt design in mind when you choose fabric. For example, for an appliquéd quilt, you need a background fabric and fabric for the appliqué pieces. Background fabrics are usually solids, light colors, or small prints that complement the appliqué design. A bold print, plaid, or stripe as a background may detract from the appliquéd design.

Wash all fabric before using to preshrink, to test for colorfastness, and to remove excess dye. Wash dark and light colors separately so that dye from dark fabrics does not run onto light fabrics. Some fabrics may require several rinses to eliminate the excess dyes. Iron fabric before cutting so that wrinkles will not distort the pieces you cut.

Tools

When you reproduce antique quilts, you don't need to use antique tools and techniques. Using rotary-cutting equipment, whenever possible, allows you to cut strips and pieces without templates. Use a self-healing mat as a cutting surface and use acrylic rulers, which are available in various sizes.

Thread

Use good-quality, strong, all-purpose cotton or cotton-covered polyester thread. For machine piecing, use a light, neutral color, such as beige or tan, for light-colored fabrics, and a dark neutral, such as dark gray, for darker fabrics.

Thread for appliqué should match the color of the appliqué pieces rather than the background fabric. If it is not possible to match the exact color of a piece, choose thread that is slightly darker than the fabric. If the appliqué fabric contains many different colors, choose a neutral-colored thread that blends with the predominant color.

Use quilting thread only for quilting. It is thicker than all-purpose thread and may show if used for piecing or appliqué.

Needles

For machine piecing, a fine needle (size 10/70) works well for most lightweight cottons. For heavier fabrics, use size 12/80.

When choosing a needle for hand appliqué, the most important consideration is the size of the needle. A fine needle will glide easily through the edges of the appliqué pieces. Sharps are for appliqué. Size 10 (fine) to size 12 (very fine) needles work well. Betweens are for quilting.

Scissors

Use your best scissors to cut fabric only, so they will stay sharp longer. Use an older pair of scissors to cut paper, cardboard, and template plastic. Small 4" scissors with sharp points are handy for clipping threads.

Marking Tools

A variety of tools is available for tracing templates onto fabric or for marking quilting lines. You can mark fabric with a regular or fine-lead mechanical pencil. Use a silver marking pencil on dark fabrics. Chalk pencils or chalk-wheel markers also work well. Test the marker you want to use on your fabric to make sure the marks can be removed easily.

Templates

Use clear or frosted plastic (available at quilting shops) to make durable, accurate templates. Templates are patterns for pieces that cannot be rotary cut. Templates for machine piecing include seam allowances. Templates for appliqué or hand piecing are made the finished size of the piece, and seam allowances are added before cutting the fabric.

Rotary Cutting

The quilt plans in this book specify rotary cutting whenever possible. Measurements for rotary cutting include standard ¼"-wide seam allowances. For those unfamiliar with rotary cutting, see the following brief introduction. For more detailed information, see Donna Thomas's *Shortcuts: A Concise Guide to Rotary Cutting.*

1. To begin cutting, fold the fabric, matching selvages and aligning the crosswise and lengthwise grains. Place the folded edge closest to you on the cutting mat. Align a square ruler along the folded edge of the fabric and place a long, straight ruler along the left edge of the square ruler, just covering the uneven raw edges of the left side of the fabric as shown. Remove the square ruler and cut along the right edge of the long ruler, moving the rotary cutter away from you as you cut. Discard the edge strip. (Reverse this procedure if you are left-handed.)

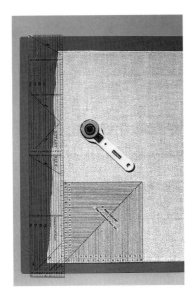

2. To cut a strip, align the desired measurement for the strip width on the ruler with the cut edge of the fabric, then cut along the ruler's edge.

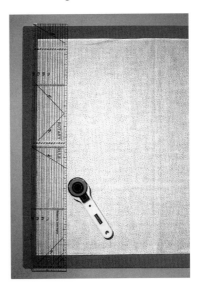

3. To cut squares, cut strips in the required widths. Trim away the selvage ends of the strip. Align the desired measurement on the ruler with the left edge of the strip and cut a square. Continue cutting squares until you have the required number. Be sure the bottom and end of the strip lines up square with the ruler before each cut.

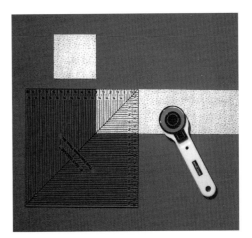

Half-Square Triangles

Half-square triangles result when you cut a square in half on the diagonal. The straight of grain is on the two short sides of each triangle. They will be on the outside edges when half-square triangle unit.

1. Cut a square, using the finished measurement of the short side of the triangle plus ⅞" for seam allowances.
2. Cut the square once diagonally, from corner to corner. Each square yields two triangles.

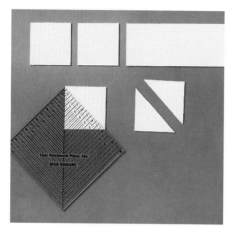

Quarter-Square Triangles

Quarter-square triangles result when a square is cut twice on the diagonal. The straight of grain is on the long side of each triangle. These long sides will be on the outside edges when you sew four triangles together to create a quarter-square unit or when they are used as side triangles in a diagonal quilt setting.

1. Cut a square, using the finished measurement of the long side of the triangle, plus 1¼" for seam allowances.
2. Cut the square twice diagonally, from corner to corner. Each square will yield four quarter-square triangles.

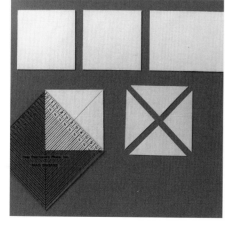

Machine Piecing

The most important thing to remember about piecing is to maintain a consistent ¼"-wide seam allowance to ensure that your quilt blocks are the desired finished size. Measurements for all components of each quilt are based on blocks that finish accurately to the desired size plus ¼" on each edge for seam allowances. Blocks that are not all the same size affect everything else in the quilt, including alternate blocks, sashings, and borders.

Take the time to establish an exact ¼"-wide seam guide on your machine. Some machines have a special quilting foot designed so that the right-hand and left-hand edges of the foot measure exactly ¼" from the center needle position. This feature allows you to use the edge of the presser foot to guide the edge of the fabric for a perfect ¼"-wide seam allowance.

If your machine doesn't have such a foot, you can create a seam guide to make it easy to stitch an accurate ¼"-wide seam allowance.

1. Place a ruler or a piece of graph paper with four squares to the inch under your presser foot.
2. Gently lower the needle onto the first ¼" line from the right edge of the ruler or paper. Place several layers of tape, a piece of moleskin, or a magnetic seam guide along the right-hand edge of the ruler or paper, so that it does not interfere with the feed dogs or presser foot. Test your new guide to make sure your seams are ¼" wide; if not, readjust your guide. *Caution: Never use a magnetic seam guide on a computerized sewing machine.*

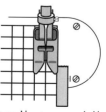

Put masking tape or moleskin
in front of needle along edge
of graph paper to guide fabric.

Appliquéing

Because so many of the quilts in this book involve appliqué, we are providing information about several popular appliqué methods.

Prepare the background for placement of appliqué shapes by centering it over the full-size paper pattern. Pin or tape the fabric in place. Using a #3 pencil or a 0.5 mechanical pencil, mark the appliqué outlines as lightly as possible onto the background fabric. Remember, every line you make must be covered or removed upon completion of the appliqué. If you mark only crucial placement points as shown in the diagram, you won't have to worry about slight variations between your appliqué shapes and the markings.

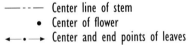
— – – – Center line of stem
• Center of flower
←–•–→ Center and end points of leaves

Freezer-Paper Appliqué (Inside Method)

1. Trace each shape to be appliquéd onto freezer paper (dull side up). Make one of these freezer-paper templates for each appliqué piece. Cut out pieces.

   NOTE: Make multiples of any shape that appears more than once by tracing the shape onto your freezer paper, stacking pieces of freezer paper (up to six layers), and cutting out several pieces at a time.

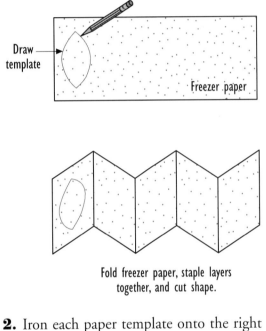

Draw template

Freezer paper

Fold freezer paper, staple layers together, and cut shape.

2. Iron each paper template onto the right side of the fabric (matte side up, coated side down). Cut out the appliqué shape, leaving ¼" all around.

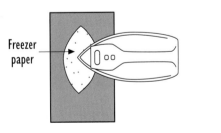
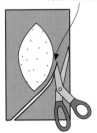

Freezer paper

¼"-wide seam allowance

3. Peel off the paper template. Place the fabric shape right side down on the ironing board. Recenter the paper shape, with the coated side up, over the fabric shape.

4. Using the point of a hot, dry iron (cotton setting), press the seam allowances to the coated side of the freezer paper. This "bastes" the seam allowance down.

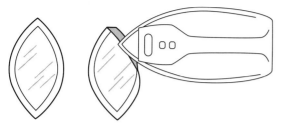

5. Place the shape in the marked location on the background and press lightly with the hot iron to "baste" it in place. Starting on a straight edge or gentle curve, stitch around the shape. Do not begin at an outside or an inside point.

6. Stop appliquéing about ½" from where you began. Pull back the seam allowance, grasp the edge of the paper, and pull it out. Finish stitching around the piece.

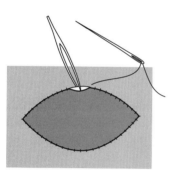

Remove freezer paper with tweezers.

NOTE: The paper can also be removed from the back by making a small slit in the background fabric behind the appliqué. Reach in and grasp the paper shape to remove it. A small tweezers works well for this.

Remove freezer paper through slit.

Needle-Turn Appliqué

1. Make sewing-line templates from template plastic or heavy paper. Trace the template shapes onto the right side of the fabric.
2. Cut out the fabric pieces, adding a scant ¼"-wide seam allowance.
3. Position the appliqué pieces on the background fabric, and pin or baste in place.
4. Beginning on a straight edge or gentle curve, use the tip of the needle to gently turn under the seam allowance a thread or two beyond the marked seam line, smoothing it out under the folded edge before sewing.
5. Turn under about a ½" length of the seam allowance at a time. Hold the turned seam allowance firmly between the thumb and first finger of your left hand (reverse if left-handed) as you stitch the appliqué to the background. Use a longer needle, a sharp, or a milliner's needle, to help you control the seam allowance and turn it under neatly.

Traditional Appliqué Stitch

The traditional appliqué stitch or blind stitch is appropriate for sewing all shapes of appliqués, including sharp points and curves.

1. Tie a knot in a single strand of thread that is approximately 18" long.
2. Hide the knot by slipping the needle into the seam allowance from the wrong side of the appliqué piece and bringing it out on the fold line.
3. Start the first stitch by moving the needle straight off the appliqué and inserting it into the background fabric. Let the needle travel under the background fabric, parallel to the edge of the appliqué, bringing it up about ⅛" away, along the edge of the shape.
4. As you bring the needle up, pierce the appliqué piece, catching only one or two threads of the folded edge.
5. Move the needle straight off the appliqué into the background fabric. Let your needle travel under the background, bringing it up about ⅛" away, again catching the edge of the appliqué. Give the thread a slight tug and continue stitching.

6. To end your stitching, pull the needle through to the wrong side. Take two small stitches behind the appliqué piece, making knots by taking your needle through the loops. Check the right side to see if the thread "shadows" through your background. If it does, take one more small stitch through the back side to direct the tail of the thread under the appliqué fabric.

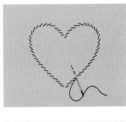

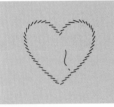

Stitching Outside Points

1. As you stitch toward an outside point, start taking smaller stitches about ½" before the point. Trim the seam allowance or push the excess fabric under the point with the tip of your needle. Smaller stitches near the point will keep frayed edges from escaping.

2. Place the last stitch before the point, very close to it. Place the next stitch very close to the point on the other side to achieve a sharp outside point.

Stitching Inside Points

1. About ½" from the point, begin making your stitches smaller.

2. Continue one stitch past the point, then return to the point to add one extra stitch exactly at the point to emphasize it. Come up through the appliqué, catching a little more fabric in the inside point (four or five threads instead of one or two). Make

a straight stitch outward, going under the point to pull it in a little and emphasize the shape of the point.

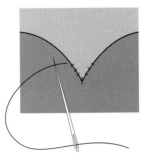

3. If your inside point frays, take a few stitches close to it to secure the fabric. If your thread matches your appliqué fabric, these stitches will blend in with the edge of the shape.

TIP: When basting any appliqué with multiple pieces, use tailor tacks at the beginning and end of each piece. Using this stitch, you don't have to knot and tie off each time; you can go from one shape to another. Remember, the secret to successful and easy appliqué is preparation.

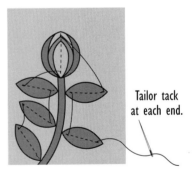

Tailor tack at each end.

Fusible Appliqué

Use paper-backed fusible web, such as Wonder-Under™, to quickly adhere appliqué pieces to a fabric background. Finish the edges with a decorative stitch or leave them unfinished. Remember that the image you get using fusible appliqué is always the reverse of the pattern image you start with.

1. Trace appliqué shapes onto the paper side of the fusible web. Cut out shapes, leaving ½" around the edges.

2. Place the fusible web shapes on the wrong side of the appliqué fabric, web side down. Press in place with a hot iron.
3. Cut the shape from the fabric on the drawn sewing line; seam allowances are not necessary.
4. Remove the paper backing.
5. Arrange the appliqué pieces on the background. Press the pieces in place with a hot iron.
6. Use a buttonhole stitch, a blanket stitch, or a satin stitch to finish the edges if desired. Stitch by hand or machine. You can leave the edges unfinished if the quilt will not be handled or washed.

Making Bias Stems

There are several ways to prepare bias strips for stems. The following bias-bar method is our favorite.

1. Cut the required number of 1½"-wide bias strips.
2. Fold a strip in half lengthwise, wrong sides together, and place your bias bar (plastic or metal) inside, against the fold, lining up the raw edges.

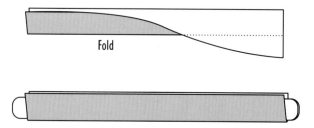

Fold

3. Stitch along the side of the bar, as close to it as possible. A zipper foot works well for this.

4. Twist the bias tube (still on the bar) so that the seam runs up the flat side of the bar.
5. Trim the seam allowance to about ⅛".

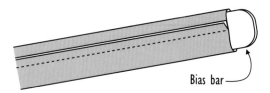

Bias bar

6. Press the tube (with bar still inside) with a hot, dry iron (cotton setting) and remove the prepared tube from the bar. Press again to get a sharp crease.
7. Use a glue stick to dab the back of the tube along the seam at 1" intervals.
8. Place the tube (glue side down) onto background fabric, centering it on the marked placement line. (The glue will hold it in place until it is basted.)
9. Baste in place with a long running stitch.
10. Begin stitching on an inner curve. Be sure that the stem lies flat and doesn't buckle.

Assembling the Quilt Top

When your blocks are complete, take the time to square them up. Use a large square ruler to measure your blocks and make sure they are the desired size plus an extra ¼" on each edge for seam allowances. For example, if you are making 6" blocks, they should all measure 6½" before you sew them together. If the sizes of the completed blocks vary greatly, trim the larger ones to match the size of the smallest one. Be sure to trim all four sides or your block will be lopsided.

Piecing your blocks accurately is important because if they are not the finished size given in the quilt plan, you must adjust all of the other components of the quilt as well.

Straight-Set Quilts

1. Arrange and sew the blocks together in rows as shown in the quilt plan, pressing the seams in opposite directions from row to row.
2. Sew the rows together, making sure to match the seams between the blocks.

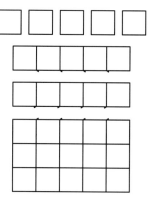

Diagonally Set Quilts

1. Arrange the blocks, side triangles, and corner triangles as shown in the quilt plan.
2. Sew the blocks together in diagonal rows and press the seams in opposite directions from row to row.
3. Sew the rows together, making sure to match the seams between the blocks. Add the corner triangles last.

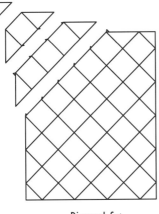

Diagonal Set

Adding the Borders

For best results, measure the quilt top across the center before adding the borders. The edges of a quilt often measure slightly longer than the distance through the quilt center due to stretching during construction. Sometimes, each side edge is a different length. Using those measurements may result in a quilt with wavy borders. Measure the quilt top through the center in both directions to determine how long to cut the border strips. This step ensures that the finished quilt will be as straight and as "square" as possible.

Plain border strips are commonly cut along the crosswise grain and pieced together to obtain the necessary length. Borders cut from the lengthwise grain of the fabric require extra yardage, but they are the least stretchy (therefore, most stable) type of border strips and require no piecing to obtain the required length.

You may add borders that have straight-cut corners or borders with mitered corners.

Borders with Straight-Cut Corners

1. Measure the length of the quilt top through the center. Cut side border strips to that measurement, piecing strips as necessary.

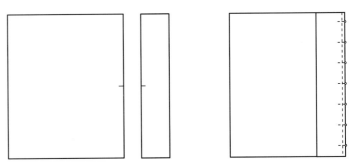

2. Mark the centers of the quilt top and the border strips. Pin the borders to the sides of the quilt top, matching the center marks and ends. Ease as necessary.
3. Sew the border strips in place. Press the seams toward the border.

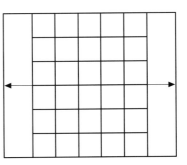

4. Measure the width of the quilt through the center, including the side borders just added. Cut border strips to that measurement, piecing strips as necessary.

5. Mark the quilt top and the border strips. Pin the borders to the top and bottom edges of the quilt top, matching the center marks and easing as necessary.

6. Sew the border strips in place. Press the seams toward the border.

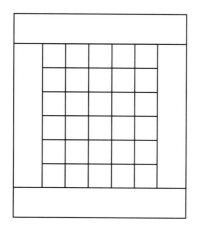

Borders with Mitered Corners

1. First estimate the finished outside dimensions of your quilt, including borders. Border strips should be cut to this length plus at least ½" for seam allowances; it's safer to add 1" to 2" to give yourself some leeway.

> **NOTE:** If your quilt is to have multiple borders, sew the individual strips together and treat the resulting unit as a single border strip. This makes mitering for corners easier and more accurate.

2. Mark the centers of the quilt edges and the centers of the border strips. Measure the length and width of the quilt across the center. Note the measurements.

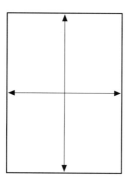

3. Place a pin at each end of the side border strips to mark the length of the quilt top. Repeat with the top and bottom borders.

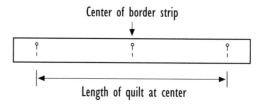

4. Stitch the borders to the quilt with a ¼"-wide seam, matching the centers; the border strip should extend the same distance at each end of the quilt. Start and stop your stitching ¼" from the corners of the quilt; press the seams toward the borders.

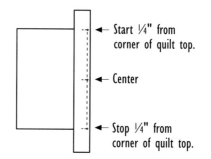

5. Lay the first corner to be mitered on the ironing board. Fold under one strip at a 45° angle and adjust so seam lines match perfectly. Press and pin.

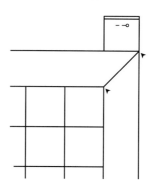

6. Fold the quilt with right sides together, lining up the edges of the border. If necessary, use a ruler to draw a pencil line on the crease to make the line more visible. Stitch on the pressed crease, sewing from the corner to the outside edge.

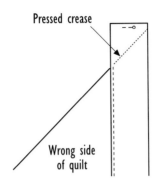

Pressed crease

Wrong side of quilt

7. Press the seam open and trim away excess border strips, leaving a ¼"-wide seam allowance.

8 . Repeat with remaining corners.

Marking the Quilt Top

Whether or not to mark the quilting designs on the quilt top depends upon the type of quilting you will be doing. Marking is not necessary if you plan to quilt in-the-ditch (close to the seam lines) or outline-quilt (a uniform distance from seam lines). Mark more complex quilting designs on the quilt top before the quilt is layered with batting and backing.

Choose a marking tool that will be visible on your fabric and test it on fabric scraps to be sure the marks can be removed easily. Masking tape works well to mark straight quilting lines. Tape only small sections at a time and remove the tape when you stop at the end of the day; otherwise, the sticky residue may be difficult to remove from the fabric.

Making the Backing

Cut the quilt backing at least 4" larger than the quilt top on all sides. For large quilts, it is usually necessary to sew two or three lengths of fabric together to make a backing of the required size. Press the backing seams open to make quilting easier.

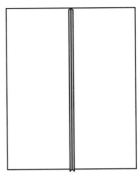

Press seam open.

Choosing the Batting

Batting comes packaged in standard bed sizes, or it can be purchased by the yard. Several weights and thicknesses are available. Thick battings are fine for tied quilts and comforters; a thinner batting is better if you intend to quilt by hand or by machine.

Thin batting is available in 100% cotton, 100% polyester, and combinations of cotton and polyester. All-cotton batting is soft and drapable but requires close quilting, while polyester and cotton/polyester battings require less quilting and are better for tied quilts.

Unroll your batting and let it relax overnight before you layer your quilt.

Layering the Quilt

1. Spread the backing, wrong side up, on a flat, clean surface. Anchor it with pins or masking tape. Be careful not to stretch the backing fabric out of shape.
2. Spread the batting over the backing, smoothing out any wrinkles.
3. Place the pressed quilt top on top of the batting. Smooth out any wrinkles and make sure the edges of the quilt top are parallel to the edges of the backing.
4. Baste with needle and thread, starting in the center and working diagonally to each corner. Continue basting in a grid of horizontal and vertical lines 6" to 8" apart. Finish by basting around the edges.

NOTE: For machine quilting, you may baste the layers with #1 rust-proof safety pins. Place pins about 4" to 6" apart, away from the area you intend to quilt.

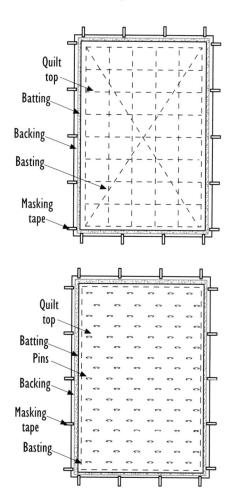

Quilting

Traditional Hand Quilting

To quilt by hand, you will need short, sturdy needles (called "Betweens"), quilting thread, and a thimble to fit the middle finger of your sewing hand. Most quilters also use a frame or hoop to support their work. Quilting needles run from size 3 to 12: the higher the number, the smaller the needle. Use the smallest needle you can comfortably handle; the smaller the needle, the smaller your stitches will be.

1. Thread your needle with a single strand of quilting thread about 18" long. Make a small knot and insert the needle in the top layer about 1" from the place where you want to start stitching. Pull the needle out at the point where quilting will begin and gently pull the thread until the knot pops through the fabric and into the batting.
2. Take small, evenly spaced stitches through all three quilt layers.
3. Rock the needle up and down through all the layers, until you have three or four stitches on the needle. Place your other hand underneath the quilt so you can feel the needle point with the tip of your finger when a stitch is taken.
4. To end a line of quilting, make a small knot close to the last stitch; then backstitch, running the thread a needle's length through the batting. Gently pull the thread until the knot pops into the batting. Clip the thread at the quilt's surface.

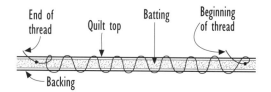

For more information on hand quilting, refer to *Loving Stitches* by Jeana Kimball.

Tying

Many antique quilts were tied together rather than quilted. It was a quicker method of finishing a quilt meant for everyday use. Today, tying gives a folk art or "homey" feel to the finished quilt.

Use perle cotton or six strands of embroidery floss and a needle with a large eye and sharp point. From the top side, go in and come back up about ¼" away, leaving a 6" tail. Tie a square knot and then another square knot for security.

Go to the next place you plan to put a knot and tie again. Cut the tails after several knots.

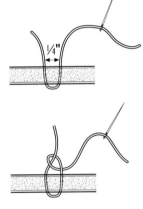

Adding Sleeves

If you plan to display your finished quilt on the wall, add a hanging sleeve before adding the binding.

1. Cut a strip of fabric 6" to 8" wide and 1" shorter than the width of the quilt at the top edge. Fold the ends under ½", then ½" again, and stitch.

2. Fold the strip in half lengthwise, wrong sides together, and baste the raw edges to the top edge of the quilt back. The top edge of the sleeve will be secured when the binding is added to the quilt.

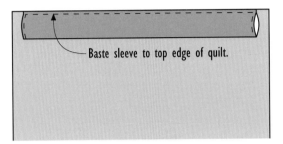

Baste sleeve to top edge of quilt.

3. Push the bottom edge of the sleeve up just a bit to provide a little room for the hanging rod. Blindstitch the bottom of the sleeve in place.

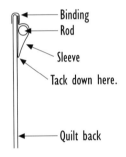

Binding
Rod
Sleeve
Tack down here.
Quilt back

Binding

Bindings can be made from straight-cut or bias-cut strips of fabric. Before applying either type of binding, trim the batting and backing even with the quilt-top edges on all sides.

Cut straight-grain binding strips 2½" wide across the width of the fabric. Cut enough strips to go around the perimeter of the quilt plus 10" for seams and corners.

To cut bias binding, fold a square of fabric on the diagonal.

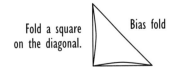

Fold a square on the diagonal.   Bias fold

OR fold a ½-yard piece of fabric as shown in the diagrams below, paying careful attention to the location of the lettered corners.

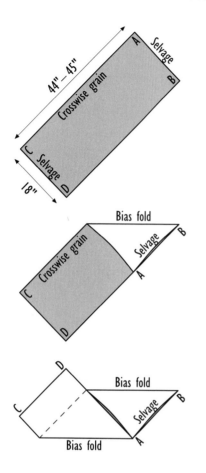

Cut 2½"-wide strips perpendicular to the folds as shown.

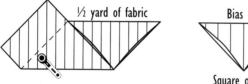

½ yard of fabric

Bias fold

Square of fabric

To attach binding:

1. Sew strips, right sides together, to make one long, continuous piece of binding. Press seams open.

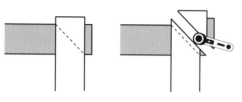

Joining Straight-Cut Strips

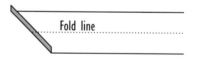

Joining Bias-Cut Strips

2. At one end of the binding strip, turn under ¼" at a 45° angle and press. Turning the end under at an angle prevents bulk where the two ends of the binding meet.

Fold line

3. Fold the binding strip in half lengthwise, wrong sides together, and press.

4. Starting on one side of the quilt, stitch the binding to the quilt, keeping the raw edges even with the quilt-top edge and using a ¼"-wide seam allowance. End the stitching ¼" from the corner of the quilt and backstitch. Clip the thread.

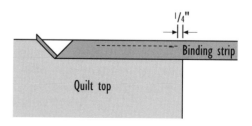

¼"

Binding strip

Quilt top

5. Turn the quilt so that you will be stitching down the next side. Fold the binding up, away from the quilt.

6. Fold the binding back down onto itself, parallel with the edge of the quilt top. Begin stitching at the edge of the quilt, backstitching to secure.

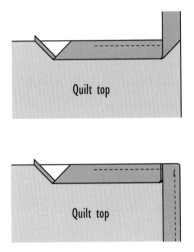

7. Continue stitching around the quilt, repeating steps 4–6 above at each of the remaining corners. Continue sewing about 1" past the point where the binding overlaps the beginning point. Trim the end at a 45° angle. Tuck the end of the binding into the fold and finish the seam.

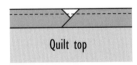

8. Fold the binding over the raw edges of the quilt to the back, with the folded edge of the binding covering the row of machine stitching, and blindstitch in place. A miter will form at each corner. Blindstitch the mitered corners in place.

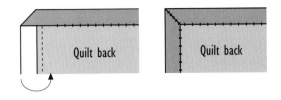

Making Labels

Labels can be as elaborate or as simple as you desire. The information can be handwritten, typed, or embroidered. Be sure to include your name, the date, the place where the quilt was made, and the person for whom it was made. Too many antique quilts are unlabeled, and the identities of their makers are forgotten.

That Patchwork Place Publications and Products

4", 6", 8", & metric Bias Square® • BiRangle™ • Ruby Beholder™ • ScrapMaster • Rotary Rule™ • Rotary Mate™ • Bias Stripper™ Ruler
Shortcuts to America's Best-Loved Quilts (video)

Many titles are available at your local quilt shop. For more information, send $2 for a color catalog to
That Patchwork Place, Inc., PO Box 118, Bothell WA 98041-0118 USA.

☎ Call 1-800-426-3126 for the name and location of the quilt shop nearest you.